Home for Christmas

Home for Christmas

Jeremy Archer

Illustrated by Matilda Hunt

Century · London

Published by Century 2007

4 6 8 10 9 7 5 3

First published in Great Britain in 2007 by
Century
Random House, 20 Vauxhall Bridge Road,
London SW1V 2SA

www.rbooks.co.uk

Addresses for companies within The Random House Group Limited can be found at:
www.randomhouse.co.uk/offices.htm

The Random House Group Limited Reg. No. 954009

A CIP catalogue record for this book
is available from the British Library

ISBN 9781846051708

The Random House Group Limited makes every effort to ensure that the papers used in its books are
made from trees that have been legally sourced from well-managed and credibly certified forests. Our
paper procurement policy can be found at: www.rbooks.co.uk/environment

Mixed Sources
Product group from well-managed
forests and other controlled sources
www.fsc.org Cert no. TT-COC-2139
© 1996 Forest Stewardship Council
FSC

Typeset by SX Composing DTP, Rayleigh, Essex
Printed and bound in Great Britain by
Clays Ltd, St Ives plc

Acknowledgments

This book – which grew out of the Christmas booklets that I write every year for our friends – would never have been published without the inspiration and intervention of my old friend Roger Field. I would also like to thank Mark Booth, Charlotte Haycock and the team at Century for their professional help and guidance as the project evolved and Julene Knox for her commendable persistence and remarkable skill in unearthing permissions. I am extremely grateful to Tilly Hunt, who has skilfully produced just the style of whimsical illustration that I had hoped for.

In this country we are fortunate in the depth of archive material available and the care and attention devoted to it: the staff at the Imperial War Museum, the National Army Museum, the British Library, the National Archives, King's College, London and West Hill Library, Wandsworth have been unfailingly helpful. I also owe an enormous debt of gratitude to those people who have had the wisdom to enhance the national collections by donating personal and family material, before permitting me to make use of it for this anthology. It has been a great privilege to have been able to learn more about many of the contributors – and their families – as a result of direct contact during my research. This book is not intended to be 'dry-as-dust' military history; it is all about the people who helped to make that history. In many instances such contact has helped me to flesh out their moving stories.

Finally, I would like to thank my wife, Amanda, for the tolerance with which she has accepted the long hours that I have spent in libraries or in my study during the last two years. This book is dedicated both to her and also to our son, Sebastian, with whom I should really have spent more time 'bonding'.

Introduction

Families have always had to endure periods of separation during wartime. No-one knew how long that separation might last: all too frequently it turned out to be permanent. In 1914 the common refrain was 'It'll all be over by Christmas'. In October 1943 Bing Crosby recorded the bitter-sweet song, 'I'll be home for Christmas'. On 24 November 1950 General Douglas MacArthur assured his troops in Korea that they would be home for Christmas dinner. Wars are unpredictable and the participants were seldom 'Home for Christmas'.

Christmas is the one day in the year when families long to gather together, to exchange gifts, to celebrate the birth of Christ and, just as importantly, to enjoy themselves. Letters and diary entries always seem to be longer at this time of year since it was important to share information about how Christmas Day was spent. Although the language has changed over the years, the sentiments have remained exactly the same: that sense of longing to be with the family and, failing that, the importance of plum-pudding, washed down with copious quantities of beer, to ease the pain of separation.

In researching this book, I have been astonished at the lengths that people have gone to – sometimes in the most desperate circumstances – to mark this most special of days. Prodigious efforts were often made to provide those in the field with seasonal fare although, as the reader will discover, this was not without its hazards. In prisoner-of-war or internment camps, provisions were hoarded for months beforehand; if there were children present as well, every effort was made to make the day as memorable as possible, with all the traditional elements: normal life temporarily recreated in a hostile environment.

Some reflected on the irony that the Christmas message – *Glory to God in the highest, and on earth peace, good will toward men* – was a source of comfort to friend and foe alike. It is also striking that, under the duress of war, Christmas brought different denominations and beliefs together. Christmas during wartime has inspired poets and politicians: the former touched by the muse – comic or tragic – while the latter sensed an opportunity to assert their leadership skills.

Wars rarely stop for Christmas and one side frequently attempts to seize the advantage should the other temporarily drop its guard. On the other hand the soldiers on the ground sometimes used their own initiative, defied orders and fraternised with the enemy. Meanwhile 'psychological operations' were often used to undermine the morale of vulnerable young men whose innermost thoughts naturally lay with home and their families.

This anthology, which covers the last 230 years, explores Christmas during times of war, in the words of the combatants of different nationalities, and also of their families. The unpolished voices of the lowest-ranking servicemen and women are here, alongside what would now be called the 'spin' of the political leaders and military commanders. Whether serving in the Peninsula, in the Crimea, in South or East Africa, on the Western Front, in northern India, in Italy, on the Home Front, in Korea, Vietnam, Afghanistan or Iraq, or being held in captivity, valiant attempts have been made – often in the most unfavourable conditions – to celebrate the birth of Christ.

1777

In General Congress on 4 July 1776, representatives of 'the thirteen United States of America' signed 'a unanimous Declaration', which included the words: 'We hold these truths to be self-evident, that all men are created equal, that they are endowed by their Creator with certain unalienable Rights, that among these are Life, Liberty and the pursuit of Happiness.' What followed was the American War of Independence, or the American Revolutionary War, depending on your point of view. In his diary Lieutenant John Peebles, a thirty-eight year-old native of Irvine, Ayrshire, serving in the 42nd, or Royal Highland, Regiment, described a Christmas spent in reasonable comfort as a member of the British forces strategically positioned both in and around Philadelphia, then the capital of Britain's American colony: [1]

Thursday 25th. Xmass. Very pleasant weather for the season — 3 days provisions come out from Town. The waggons still busy carrying home forage — this morng. the Light horse kill'd 3, wounded 2 & took 5 of the Rebels — some Battalions moved further down on the Chester road to cover the waggons below Darby Creek — The firing yesterday, was betwixt our lines & some Row Galleys that came down the River — Xmas not entirely forgot.

[1] *John Peebles' American War 1776–1782*, edited by Ira D. Gruber, published by the Army Records Society in 1998: reprinted by kind permission of the Army Records Society.

1777

Baron Johann DeKalb was originally from Bavaria and, at the age of sixteen, joined the French Army as a soldier of fortune. Having been recruited to the rebel cause during the American War of Independence, DeKalb and the Marquis de Lafayette landed at Georgetown, South Carolina on 14 June 1777. Both were appointed major-general by the Continental Congress. Unlike the British forces, Washington's army was in a distressing predicament at Valley Forge, Pennsylvania, as Baron DeKalb described in his Christmas Day letter to Comte de Broglie:[2]

On the 19th instant the army reached this wooded wilderness, certainly one of the poorest districts of Pennsylvania; the soil thin, uncultivated, and almost uninhabited, without forage and without provisions! Here we are to go into winter-quarters, i.e., to lie in shanties, generals and privates, to enable the army, it is said, to recover from its privations, to recruit, to re-equip, and to prepare for the opening of the coming campaign while protecting the country against hostile inroads . . .

It is unfortunate that Washington is so easily led. He is the bravest and truest of men, has the best intentions, and a sound judgment. I am convinced that he would accomplish substantial results, if he would only act more upon his own responsibility; but it is a pity that he is so weak, and has the worst of advisers in the men who enjoy his confidence. If they are not traitors, they are certainly gross ignoramuses . . .

I do not know what is done in the clothing department; but it is certain that half the army are half naked, and almost the whole army go barefoot . . . Our men are also infected with the itch, a matter which attracts very little attention either at the hospitals or in camp. I have seen the poor fellows covered over and over with scab. I have caused my seven regiments to put up barracks large

[2] *The Life of John Kalb, Major-General in the Revolutionary War* by Friedrich Kapp, published by Henry Holt and Company, New York in 1884. On 26 June 1950 President Harry S. Truman told the South Korean Ambassador to the United States: 'Many years ago, when Americans were fighting for their independence, at Valley Forge, our soldiers lacked food, medicine, clothing. Then some friends came and helped.'

enough to hold all these unfortunates, so that they can be subjected to medical treatment away from the others.

All things seem to contribute to the ruin of our cause. If it is sustained, it can only be by a special interposition of Providence. The army contractors have been consulted as to the best place for going into winter-quarters, and have declared that the present location is the most convenient for them. This, bye-the-bye, was done contrary to my advice. Now we have hardly been here six days, and are already suffering for want of everything. The men have had neither meat nor bread for four days, and our horses are often left for days without any fodder. What will be done when the roads grow worse, and the season more severe?

Baron Johann DeKalb was killed at the battle of Camden on 16 August 1780. On 2 September 1780 his aide-de-camp, Lieutenant-Colonel le Chevalier Charles-François du Buysson des Hays, wrote:[3]

The Baron DeKalb, deserted by all the militia, who fled at the first fire, withstood with the greatest bravery, coolness and intrepidity, with the brave Marylanders alone, the furious charge of the whole British army; but superior bravery was obliged at length to yield to superior numbers, and the baron, having had his horse killed under him, fell into the hands of the enemy, pierced with eight wounds of bayonets and three musket balls. I stood by the baron during the action and shared his fate, being taken by his side, wounded in both arms and hands. Lord Cornwallis and Rawdon treated us with the greatest civility. The baron, dying of his wounds two days after the action, was buried with all the honors of war, and his funeral attended by all the officers of the British army. The doctor having reported to Lord Cornwallis the impossibility of curing my wounds in that part of the continent, he admitted me to my parole, to go to Philadelphia for effecting an exchange between me and Lieut.-Col. Hamilton &c.

---

[3] *Historic Camden, Colonial and Revolutionary, Volume 1* by Thomas J. Kirkland and Robert M. Kennedy, published by The State Company, Columbia in 1905. Six American states have counties named after Baron Johann DeKalb: Alabama, Georgia, Indiana, Illinois, Missouri and Tennessee. Unsurprisingly, George Washington heads the list, with thirty-one States; Thomas Jefferson is in second position with twenty-six while Benjamin Franklin is third, with twenty-five.

1781

On 19 October 1781 Lord Cornwallis surrendered the 7,000-strong British garrison at Yorktown to Washington, Rochambeau and Lafayette, leading to the resignation of British Prime Minister, Lord North, when he heard the shocking news of the capitulation. Despite British control of major ports such as New York and Charleston, the war was effectively over by Christmas that year. Captain John Peebles was now stationed on Long Island: [4]

Tuesday 25th. Xmass The ground cover'd with snow as usual at this Season of mirth & festivity, & the sleighs flying about. Our Mess being engaged to dine with the Mess over the way, we met at the usual hour vizt. 4 o'clock sat down to a good dinner and took hearty drink, which is to be repeated at our Mess on New Years day. With some intermediate drinks with other people, in this manner we live & go on, trying to procure pleasure at the expense of the constitution.

Sensing, perhaps, the futility of the continued presence of the British Army in North America, John Peebles sold his King's Commission to Lieutenant William Dickson on 8 February 1782. Having said farewell to his company and made a 'little speech, my voice faulter'd, and my knees shook under me', he booked a passage on a ship bound for Glasgow and sailed on 2 March. John Peebles later became surveyor for the port of Irvine and died in 1823, at the age of eighty-four.

---

[4] *John Peebles' American War 1776–1782*, Ibid.

1803

John Pester was born on 22 December 1778 at Odcombe, Somerset, was appointed ensign in the Bengal Army on 5 September 1800 and arrived in India on 8 December that year. He joined the 2nd Bengal Native Infantry and was heavily engaged during the Second Maratha (or Mahratta) War, taking part in the siege of Sasni, suffering wounds at Kachaura, and leading his Grenadiers at the battle of Delhi on 11 September 1803 and the capture of Agra on 20 October 1803. Lieutenant John Pester was appointed Brigade Major, 4th Brigade on 26 October 1803. That Christmas was spent in camp at Jettowr on the banks of the river Chumbill:[5]

The Brigade halted to-day, and it being Christmas Day, extra batta[6] was served out to the Europeans in our camp; here we procured a good supply of flour and grain. The land was poor and thinly cultivated, except on spots near the villages. Received letters to-day by an express from the Grand Army, from Wemyss and Maling; the former gave me information of the arrival of the 'Tigress' and three Company's ships from England, and sent me the heads of intelligence brought out by them. Dined at home to-day, and the Brigadier gave an immense dinner to nearly all the officers off duty in camp.[7] We sat up late, and drank a good deal of claret; a great number of songs were sung, and we parted at a late hour.

John Pester later took part in the capture of Gwalior on 5 February 1804 and the capture of Deig on 24 December 1804 (see next entry). Out of

---

[5] *War and Sport in India — An Officer's Diary*, edited by J. A. Devenish, published by Heath, Crane & Ouseley Ltd, in 1912.

[6] Batta – an extra allowance made to officers, soldiers, or other public servants, when in the field, or on other special grounds.

[7] The Brigadier in question, Henry (later Sir Henry) White, went further in John Pester's case, leaving him £500 in his will in grateful acknowledgement of the assistance that he had given at the siege of Gwalior.

eighteen officers of the 1st Battalion, 2nd Native Infantry, only three were fit for duty at the close of the gruelling 1804 campaign. In April 1811 he married Elizabeth, elder daughter of the Reverend William Phelips of Montacute House, near Yeovil. John Pester retired from the Honourable East India Company's Army as a lieutenant-colonel on 6 January 1826, lived to receive his Army of India medal with three bars in 1851 and died on 1 August 1856 at Millbrook, near Southampton.

1804

James Young was born on 2 October 1782, the son of John Young, Professor of Greek at Glasgow University. Appointed to the Bengal Army, he arrived in India on 25 October 1801, was promoted lieutenant on 25 February 1802 and served with the 1st Troop, Horse Artillery during the Maratha War 1804–05. In his excitement, the fact that it was Christmas Day completely escaped him:[8]

25th — This morning we were fortunate enough to see the Union Jack of Great Britain flying on the walls of the Fort of Deeg, which had been evacuated during the night by it's Garrison. Suspecting, from the attempts at correspondence made by the Enemy, that they would do something of the kind during the Night, His Exc[y], most prudently, did not by attempting to take the place by force, throw away the lives of his men. When day broke it was found Empty & instantly occupied by us. After breakfast almost the whole Camp went down to visit the fort & Town. I, among the Number, went over the whole of the Trenches, Batteries, Enemy's Lines, Forts, Shah Boorj & City . . . The New & beautiful Palace of the Rajah, built on arches in a Lake, stands just without the Fort, & is, with it's beautiful Gardens, by far superior, in every respect, to any building I have seen in India. The grandeur, & heavy magnificence, of the Principal Building is indeed great & splendid. Successive tiers of Apartments descend with their Balconies into the Water, habitable as the increasing heat of the Weather dries up the Tanks. The Zenana or Daftarkhanna both built in part of marble, beautifully worked & carved are each, fine wings to the main building in their several styles. But what constitutes the superior Charm of this sweet place is the complete set of Jets d'Eau which border every walk in the Garden & play round every part of the Palace. There are of these many hundreds, all of them supplied by a large Deep quadrangular Cistern, a Bath, on the Roof of the Zenanah surrounded on the inside by holes, stopped with wooden Pegs each communicating by long pipes built in the Walls with it's Jet so that on the removal of a peg, its Corresponding Fountain instantly begins Playing. The Cistern itself is recruited by Water; drawn

---

[8] *The Second Maratha Campaign 1804–1805*, edited by D. D. Khanna, Allied Publishers Pvt Ltd, New Delhi in 1990: by kind permission of the publishers.

up from the surrounding Tanks. Whilst I was there the secret of the Pegs was discovered, & we in a few minutes let most of these beautiful Fountains a flowing. The Effect was beautiful & gratifying beyond belief & reminded one of the Sultans, in the Arabian Nights Entertainments repairing with their Favourites of women to their Groves & Gardens surrounded by running streams & playing fountains while the Guest, the song, the Dance, the story 'went merrily round'.

James Young later served as Military Secretary to the 1st Marquess of Hastings, Governor-General of India, as Secretary to the Law Commission and as first non-official Sheriff of Calcutta. He died on 17 August 1848 at Boulogne-sur-Mer.

1807/10

On 22 February 1806 Peter Bussell 'parted from a fond wife and two young children, with the greatest spirits, not dreaming how soon the fate of a cruel war would upset my well-planned schemes'. He was part-owner of the 70-ton sloop *Dove*, which was sailing from its home port of Weymouth to London, when it was intercepted by the French privateer *Les Deux Frères*, off the Needles. The captured crew were landed at Cherbourg and marched 334 miles to Arras, where they were imprisoned in the Citadelle. Peter Bussell was eventually to list the crews of no less than 166 ships that were kept captive with him. Despite early hopes of an exchange of prisoners, Bussell was still at Arras two years later: [9]

December 25th. Being Christmas Day myself and my two mess-mates enjoyed ourselves as well as our situation would allow of. The Citadel this day seems to be all alive amongst the prisoners, the Commandant has given permission for them to have lights in their rooms all the night, and go to the Canteen any time they think proper. A great number was drunk before their dinner was ready, so that their enjoyment of the day was but little.

Three years later there was still no change in Peter Bussell's circumstances, although life was made slightly more bearable by the early-Nineteenth Century equivalent of *Red Cross* parcels:

December the 25th. Being Christmas Day the greatest part of the prisoners are enjoying themselves as well as their little means will admit of. Many, before seven in the morning, had a skin full of brandy. Myself, with others of my unfortunate townsmen, was this day paid part of a subscription from our benevolent benefactors at Weymouth.

[9] *The Diary of Peter Bussell*, published by Peter Davies in 1931. The *Dove* was wrecked on Chesil Beach, Dorset on 28 November 1838.

On 31 August 1811 the prisoners were 'chained by the neck, four on a chain' and marched from Arras to the Depôt at Briançon. Two years later Peter Bussell left Briançon and was marched all over northern France until he was freed in Rennes on Easter Sunday, 10 April 1814. Ten days later, Bussell travelled by the schooner *Le Messager* from St. Malo to Jersey, from where he sailed to Poole on the *Courier*. He had been away eight years and two months. Sadly his wife had died but 'the chains of captivity are burst, and I am again restored to the blessings of Liberty in my native country, where the Tree of Liberty not only blossoms, but bears its fruit'. Peter Bussell died in 1850, at the age of seventy-six.

1811

Sam's Christmas Pudding
by Marriott Edgar[10]

It was Christmas Day in the trenches
In Spain in t'Peninsular War,
And Sam Small were cleaning his musket
A thing as he'd ne'er done before.

They'd had 'em inspected that morning
And Sam had got into disgrace,
For when t'Sergeant had looked down t'barrel
A sparrow flew out in his face.

The Sergeant reported the matter
To Lieutenant Bird then and there.
Said t'Lieutenant, 'How very disgusting
The Duke must be told of this 'ere.'

The Duke were upset when he heard it.
He said, 'I'm astonished, I am,
I must make a most drastic example:
There'll be no Christmas pudding for Sam.'

When Sam were informed of 'is sentence
Surprise rooted 'im to the spot.
'Twas much worse than he had expected,
He thought as he'd only be shot.

And so he sat cleaning 'is musket
And polishing t'barrel and butt.
While the pudding his mother had sent him,
Lay there on t'grass at 'is foot.

Now the front line that Sam's lot were holding
Ran all round a town: Badajoz.[11]
Where the Frenchies 'ad put up a bastion
And ooh . . . what a bastion it was.

They pounded away all the morning
With canister, grapeshot and ball.
But the face of the bastion defied 'em,
They made no impression at all.

They started again after dinner
Bombarding as hard as they could.
And the Duke brought his own private cannon
But that weren't a ha'pence o' good.

The Duke said, 'Sam, put down thy musket
And help me lay this gun real true.'
Sam answered, 'You'd best ask your favours
From them as you give pudding to.'

The Duke looked at Sam so reproachful,
'And don't take it that way,' said he,
'Us Generals have got to be ruthless,
It hurts me more than it did thee.'

Sam sniffed at these words kind of sceptic,
Then looked down the Duke's private gun,
And said, 'We'd best put in two charges,
We'll never bust bastion with one.'

He tipped t'cannonball out of t'muzzle,
He took out the wadding and all,
He filled t'barrel chock full o' powder,
Then picked up and put back the ball.

He took a good aim at the bastion
Then said, 'Right-oh, Duke, let her fly.'
The cannon nigh jumped off its trunnions,
And up went the bastion, sky high.

The Duke, he weren't 'alf elated
He danced around t'trench full o' glee.
And said, 'Sam, for this gallant action
You can hot up your pudding for tea.'

Sam looked 'round to pick up his pudding
But it weren't there – nowhere about.
In t'place where he thought he had left it,
Lay the cannonball he'd just tipped out.

Sam saw in a flash what'd happened:
By an unprecedented mishap
The pudding his mother had sent him
Had blown Badajoz off t'map.

That's why Grenadiers wear to this moment
A badge which they think's a grenade.
But they're wrong . . . it's a brass reproduction
Of the pudding Sam's mother once made.

[10] Marriott Edgar (1880–1951), master of the monologue, who is perhaps best-known for *The Lion and Albert*. Words by George Marriott Edgar and music by Dudley Bayford © 1949, reproduced by permission of Francis Day & Hunter Ltd, London WC2H 0QY.
[11] There is some poetic licence here since Badajoz was finally captured by Wellington's army on 7 April 1812 after a short and bloody siege, having also been besieged the previous year, but never over Christmas.

1811

Lieutenant Robert Knowles was born on 4 April 1790, the fourth son of Robert Knowles of Eagley Bank, Little Bolton, Lancashire. In 1809 he was gazetted as lieutenant in the Royal Lancaster Regiment and, on 7 May 1811, he was appointed lieutenant in the 7th (Royal) Fusiliers, arriving in Lisbon in the *Matilda* on 21 August the same year. On 31 December 1811 he wrote to his father from Villa de Serva:[12]

The Army is still in the same quarters, but we are daily expecting a move. It is supposed that Ciudad Rodrigo will be Lord Wellington's first object, as he is making preparations for a siege . . . I have not heard from home since the 30th Sept., but suppose your letters must have miscarried. I did not neglect drinking your good health on Christmas Day, nor that of all my absent friends, but must say I envied their situation sitting by a fireside with their bellys full of Christmas pyes, but if they are feasting upon all the luxurys England can afford I shall enjoy them the more when I return, with this satisfaction, that I have fought for my country abroad. While writing the above I received a pressing invitation from Capt. King, of our Regiment, to dine with him and Major Despard. The only news I can give you is that we shall break ground before Ciudad Rodrigo on the 13th inst., for you must know it is now the New Year, and I have the satisfaction to wish you every pleasure this world can afford. If I do not hear from you in answer to a letter of the 8th October in a few days, I shall be under the necessity of drawing a bill upon you for £20.[13] The last letter I wrote you was of the 3rd ult., but have no doubt you have received it by this time. The Army is not so sickly as it was when I last wrote, and it gives me great pleasure to say I remain in perfect health. I will again write you if anything particular occurs.

[12] *The War in the Peninsula — Some Letters of Lieutenant Robert Knowles of the 7th, or Royal, Fusiliers, a Bolton Officer*, arranged and annotated by his great-great-nephew Sir Lees Knowles, Bart, published by Tillotson & Son Ltd in 1913.
[13] On 23 September 1812 he wrote that 'the Army was six months in arrear of pay, which must be sufficient to show you at once my situation'.

On 6 April 1812 Robert Knowles was slightly wounded in the storming of Badajoz when his 'sword hand [was] much cut and bruised' and further wounded at the Battle of Salamanca on 22 July when he 'received a musquet [sic] ball' in his left arm. After a spell of recuperation, Robert Knowles rejoined the 7th Fusiliers, only to be killed in action during the encounter battle at Roncesvalles in the Pyrénées on 25 July 1813.

1811/12

William Swabey was born on 13 June 1789, the third and youngest son of Maurice Swabey of Langley Marish, Buckinghamshire, Chancellor of the Diocese of Rochester. Commissioned on 1 July 1806, he was present at the bombardment of Copenhagen in 1807 and went to the Peninsula in July 1811. That Christmas was spent at Salguiero: [14]

Xmas Day. — Killed three snipe. Captain Bull did not come over, the rest of the party dined and slept with us. I cannot say I enjoyed my Christmas dinner, nor are these parties at all suited to my taste. This is only the second time in my life that I have been absent from our family party on this day, last year I felt more satisfaction in being so than I do this.

On 2 December 1812 with E Troop, Royal Horse Artillery, he 'marched into our cantonment at San Payo, an inconvenient dirty village without forage, on the high road from Coimbra. The quarter falling to me by my own arrangement for the winter, is an empty room with a through draught from two windows with only shutters, certainly built in the dog-days. I was luckily never born to be nice.' On Christmas Eve 'the rain ceasing for a time, I was over-persuaded to join the Major and Harding and set out with them for Taboa'. Christmas that year was no better than the previous one:

25th December — Having ridden thus far to spend Christmas Day, I could not enjoy myself because I thought only of how it had been passed in the preceding years of my life; it was always before a time of pleasure.

[14] *Diary of Campaigns in the Peninsula, for the years 1811, 12, and 13 by Lieutenant William Swabey, an officer of E Troop, Royal Horse Artillery*, edited by Colonel F. A. Whinyates, late RHA.

At the battle of Vittoria on 21 June 1813 William Swabey received a musket ball in his knee – it was never extracted. He recovered from his wounds in time for the battle of Toulouse in 1814 and later took part in the retreat from Quatre Bras and the battle of Waterloo itself. In 1820 he married Marianne, third daughter of Edward Hobson of Somerly, Hampshire – she bore him eleven children. In 1840 they emigrated to Prince Edward's Island, returning to England twenty-one years later. William Swabey served as a Deputy Lieutenant and Justice of the Peace for Buckinghamshire and died on 6 February 1872.

1812

In April 1809 William Wheeler, having 'escaped from the Militia without being flead alive', volunteered for the 51st Light Infantry. He first saw action in the Walcheren expedition the same year and arrived at Lisbon in March 1811, after which he fought at the first siege of Badajoz, the Battle of Fuentes de Oñoro and also at Salamanca on 22 July 1812. That autumn Wellington's army retreated from Burgos to Moimento, from where Wheeler wrote home on 13 January 1813:[15]

We have spent a very comfortable Christmass [sic], you know I am one of these sort of mortals that do not stand to niceties. Youth and health with a moderate share of the good things of this world always satisfies me. I have often spent many happy hours, when on the out lying picquet, when sitting by the fire smoking my pipe and listening to the marvellous tales of my comrades. But here we are a distance from the enemy, we get our rations regular and we can purchase every eatable very cheap, so is tobacco. I mention this because I know you will be pleased that we have it in our power to make ourselves comfortable after so arduous a campaign as our last was.

Lord Wellington has issued an order to the army from which he does not seem any way pleased with the conduct of the army on the Burgos retreat. I must confess that although there are some severe remarks imbodied in the orders, yet I cannot say they are uncalled for. It is impossible for any army to have given themselves up to more dissipation and everything that is bad, as did our army. The conduct of some men would have disgraced savages, drunkenness had prevaled [sic] to such a frightful extent that I have often wondered how it was that a great part of our army were not cut off. It was no infrequent thing to see a long string of mules carrying drunken soldiers to prevent them falling into the hands of the enemy. It would not be fair in me to mention any particular Corps, all partook in some degree a share of the disgrace. At Validolid, the — was punishing several hours, the sides of the roads were strewed with soldiers as if dead, not so much by fatigue as by wine. But there is some excuse, from Burgos to Salamanca is chiefly a wine

[15] *The Letters of Private Wheeler 1809–1828* edited by Sir Basil Liddell-Hart, published in 1951: reproduced by permission of David Higham Associates Ltd.

country and as there had been a good harvest, and the new wine was in tanks particularly about Validolid the soldiers ran mad. I remember seeing a soldier fully accoutred with his knapsack on in a large tank, he had either fell in or had been pushed in by his comrades, there he lay dead. I saw a Dragoon fire his pistol into a large vat containing several thousands of gallons, in a few minutes we were up to our knees in wine fighting like tigers for it.

Wheeler was badly wounded at the Battle of Nivelle in November 1813, fought at Waterloo and retired with a pension of 1s 10d per day in June 1828.

1841

Florentia, Lady Sale, wife of Major-General Sir Robert 'Fighting Bob' Sale, second-in-command of the army of occupation in Afghanistan, spent an anxious Christmas in Kabul. Her husband, who had already left the city with his brigade, with orders to clear the route to Peshawar, reached Jellalabad on 12 November, only to find himself trapped there. On 23 December 1841 Sir William Macnaughton, the Viceroy's Envoy, and Captain Robert Trevor, commander of the Hazirbash – or King's Life Guards – were killed during a parley with Akbar Khan in Kabul and their bodies left 'hanging in the public chouk'. Lady Sale wrote in her journal:[16]

A dismal Christmas day, and our situation far from cheering. A letter brought in from Conolly to say, that the Nawaub Zeman Khan had interested himself greatly in the cause, and had procured the two bodies to be stolen, and that they hoped to be able to send them in at night.[17] Trevor's had not been mutilated. It appears probable that the Envoy's death was not contemplated. Akbar wished to seize him, in hopes, by making him a hostage, to obtain better terms: but he is a man of violent passions; and, being thwarted, the natural ferocity of his disposition was evinced. At night there was some firing, and the bugles sounded; all went to their respective posts, but the party of about 200 Affghans went away. There was evidently great commotion in the city at the same time. A cossid came in from Jellalabad; but no news later than the 7th.[18]

Meanwhile Ensign Granville George Chetwynd-Stapylton, 13th Light Infantry, was a member of Sir Robert Sale's brigade, under siege in Jellalabad. On 2 January 1842 he wrote home:[19]

[16] *A Journal of the Disasters in Affghanistan, 1841–42*, published by John Murray in 1843. Chouk – market-place.
[17] Captain John Conolly, liaison officer with Shah Soojah.
[18] Cossid – a foot messenger.
[19] Published by kind permission of Lieutenant-Colonel Richard Chetwynd-Stapylton.

Our regular communication with Peshawar is not open and only a few letters have arrived here by horseman. We have, however, the pleasing intelligence that four regiments have arrived in Peshawar on their way to our relief. We are now comfortable enough as our defences are finished, and we have three months provisions on half rations . . . I dare say you will get exaggerated accounts of the business in England, but I think we shall manage to get out of the scrape somehow or other. We are all in very good spirits here, considering circumstances, spent a tolerably pleasant Christmas. Our band did not come in to play as all our music was lost and our band-master badly wounded.

The decision was taken to evacuate Kabul and, on 6 January 1842, some 4,300 soldiers and over 12,000 camp followers took the road through the Khurd Kabul Pass for India – and safety. Though her son-in-law, Captain John Sturt, Bengal Engineers, was mortally wounded on 8 January, Lady Sale wrote: 'I had, fortunately, only one ball in my arm.' Known to her husband's fellow officers as 'the Grenadier in petticoats', Florentia Sale was taken hostage by the Afghans and kept captive for the next nine months. An 'Army of Retribution' under Major-General George Pollock was assembled at Peshawar and finally relieved Jellalabad on 16 April 1842. The band of the 13th Light Infantry – now evidently recovered – left the city and accompanied them for the last few miles playing, rather appropriately, 'Oh, but ye've been lang o'coming'.

On 21 December 1845 'Fighting Bob' died of wounds received three days earlier at the battle of Moodkee, during the First Sikh War. After his death, Florentia Sale lived for some years on a small estate in the hills near Simla, before going to South Africa for her health. She died at Cape Town on 6 July 1853 and is buried there, with the following epitaph: 'Underneath this stone reposes all that could die of Lady Sale.' Their widowed daughter, Alexandrina, later married Major James Garner Holmes: on 24 July 1857 they were both beheaded in their carriage at Sagauli by four mutineers from the 12th Irregular Native Cavalry.

1841

On the morning of Christmas Eve, Lieutenant Robertson, 25th Native Infantry, had brought 'the astounding intelligence of the outbreak at Kabul, and the critical state of affairs in Affghanistan'. The Assistant Chaplain takes up the story: [20]

We spent a rather melancholy Christmas Eve, contrasting our loneliness in the old ruined factory, with the cheerful doings of days by-gone, and unable to rise immediately above the stunning effect of Mr. Robertson's news in the morning. I found (as in such cases I have always done) great relief from commending the absent friends whom the season recalled to mind, the affairs of the country, and my own, to the protection of the God of Providence, who cares alike for states and individuals.

On the following morning (Christmas Day) we rode to the Bunder, six miles. The first view of the far-famed and classic Indus was not very imposing, for the effect of its width was destroyed by a large sand-bank in the middle. Where our tent was afterwards pitched, on its bank, it appeared to me about the width of the Thames at Greenwich. At this season of the year, the stream is much lower than at others, and although widening greatly at some of its turns, I should not estimate its average width at this time, between Tattah and Sukkur, to be greater than that of the Thames at Blackwell, even if it be quite so wide. The shore opposite the Bunder very much resembled the low swampy shore of the Thames on the Kent side, opposite the East India Docks, where pirates on the high seas used to be hanged in chains; but it wanted the bold back-ground of the Kent and Surrey hills, and presented a dead sandy flat, as far as the eye could reach. The stream here was as smooth as a mill-pond, with here and there a slight eddying ripple. A detachment of HM 40th Regiment was waiting for conveyance, which assembled, on my arrival, for divine service, and I gave them a few words of exhortation on the christian method of spending Christmas Day. The service was necessarily brief, for the sun was scorching hot, and we were in the open air. This was the first time that I had ever officiated in the open air on shore. For many

[20] *Diary of a March through Sinde and Affghanistan, etc.* by The Rev I. N. Allen, BA, Assistant Chaplain on the Honourable East India Company's Bombay Establishment, published by J. Hatchard and Son, 187 Piccadilly in 1843.

months after, I had no other canopy but the sky. In the course of the morning the Satellite steamer arrived. In the evening we all dined together, seven in number, and drank the health of friends at home with deep feeling, if not with much mirth. The captain of the steamer was a man of considerable natural talent, and various and heterogeneous information, picked up here and there, and the conversation took a metaphysical turn, which I had little expected.

1842

The following Christmas Isaac Allen recorded his relief that the campaign had been concluded successfully:[21]

On the 25th December, Sunday and Christmas Day, the European troops of the Kandahar force were assembled at eight A.M. for divine service, in the centre of the camp, whom I addressed from Luke ii 11–14, and spoke of the peace which God had graciously restored to us, and the motives to thankfulness arising from the contrast between our situation on this, and the last Christmas, the very time at which the commencement of hostilities in Kabul sent them forth under arms from Tattah. At half-past ten, I went to the governor-general's tent to assist his chaplain, the Reverend Mr. Whiting, from whom I had received much kind attention. Here was a good congregation, and after morning service, we administered the Holy Communion to about forty communicants, amongst whom were the governor-general and the commander-in-chief. I was delighted to see so large a number of young officers among the recipients of the Holy Sacrament. In the afternoon, I had divine service as usual in the mess-tent of HM 40th Regiment, (only twice prevented during the campaign,) and preached from Nehemiah viii 10. After our weary marches, and distracted kind of life, these were calm and refreshing services indeed!

The Reverend Isaac Nicholas Allen died at Poona on 23 April 1853.

[21] *Diary of a March through Sinde and Affghanistan, etc.* Ibid.

1844/47

Lieutenant Maximilian Montagu Hammond, The Rifle Brigade, was posted to Halifax in Canada, from where he wrote on 2 December 1844 to his sister:[22]

How I long to be with you all at Christmas, but it is no use thinking of these things when they are impossible . . . We have had the most beautiful winter here that has been known for twenty years. Fancy a sky without a cloud, a warm sun, the thermometer at 15° or 20°, with dry hard ground without snow to walk upon, and you have before you the beauties of a blue-nose winter, of which we have had nothing else yet. But fancy a dark, black day, a stormy northerly wind, no sun, and the thermometer at 0°, up to your knees in snow, and drifting so that you can hardly see a yard before you, with your nose and chin in danger of being frost-bitten, and you have the dark side of the picture. This is all to be expected.

Two weeks later he wrote to his father:

It is now nearly Christmas, and I can hardly believe that this will be the third that I have passed in America. But I feel happier now than I have ever before; and although I should like, above all things, to spend Christmas at home, I feel that I shall enjoy it here very much.

In January 1848 he wrote from Kingston, Ontario:

My Christmas was a very pleasant one, &c., &c. Our own men had a grand dinner of capital roast beef and mutton, with plum-pudding in abundance. I wish you could have seen the splendid decorations of some of their rooms, with all kinds of devices in fir round the walls — flags, paintings, &c.; altogether the day passed off quietly, and the poor soldiers were much pleased.

[22] *Memoir of Captain M. M. Hammond, Rifle Brigade*, published by Robert Carter & Brothers in New York in 1858.

In April 1854 Captain 'Maxy' Hammond departed from England for service in the Crimean War. Taken ill as soon as he arrived, he was evacuated to the hospital at Scutari in early September, and then by steamer to England on 15 October 1854. After recuperating for ten months, he arrived back in the Crimea on 5 September 1855. Just three days later – his first day of service in the Crimea – 'Maxy' Hammond took part in the last battle of the Crimean War: another assault on the heavily-defended Redan. At 6.30 a.m. on 8 September he concluded a final letter to his wife:

I have had a peaceful time for prayer, and have committed the keeping of my soul and body to the Lord my God, and have commended to His grace and care my wife and child, my parents, brothers and sisters, and all dear to me. Come what will, all is well. This day will be a memorable one. Farewell, once more! Ps. XCI 15 is my text for today, especially the words, 'I will be with him in trouble.'

A few minutes later 'Maxy' Hammond fell under 'a forest of Russian bayonets'.

1848

Daniel George Robinson was commissioned into the Bengal Engineers, Honourable East India Company's Army in June 1843. On 31 December 1848 he wrote to his father from Shamsabad in Hazara, now one of the districts of North-West Frontier Province, Pakistan:[23]

I spent Xmas Day at Peshawur [sic] *where we assembled five Europeans & had a quiet sedate dinner returning the next day but one stopping the Sunday. The Peshawur country is curious, the inhabitants are genuine Affghans* [sic] *& it is tilled & irrigated in a peculiar way much resembling the Affghan principle . . . In England you thought me irreligious & tolerably wild but though not far from wrong I have always had an inclination toward religion & I can assure you I never saw a Christian service attended with more apparent zeal that it was by five young men on Xmas day & the Sunday after at Peshawur the other day. I find that the society of young men in the army generally contaminates but that where there is knowledge & understanding religion is generally carried far and the characters are more formed & steady.*

At Mussoorie in September 1851 Daniel Robinson married Jane Amelia Graham: they had nine children and six of the boys joined either the British Army or the Indian Army. Daniel Robinson served as Director-General of Telegraphs in India from 1865 to 1877 but, with his health broken by the rigours of life on the sub-continent, died in the P&O steamer *Travancore* on 27 July 1877, while on his way back to England.

---

[23] *Military Miscellany I* – Army Records Society, edited by Alan J. Guy, R. N. W. Thomas and Gerard J. DeGroot, published in 1997: reprinted by kind permission of the Army Records Society.

1854

In 1897 my great-grandfather, William Allan, finally succumbed to pressure from his second wife and published what he referred to as his 'old rubbish', which included his letters from the Crimea to his family in Edinburgh. A lieutenant in the 41st Regiment (later The Welch Regiment), he had fought at the battles of the Alma and Inkerman and was encamped before Sebastopol, from where he wrote on 26 December:[24]

We passed rather a pleasant Christmas Day yesterday, considering everything; it was a lovely day, with hard frost in the morning. I have knocked up a small kitchen hut, and eight of us dined together in it. Lord Raglan presented Kingscote with a goose, which was a most welcome addition to our rations of fresh meat, *which they managed to serve out to the troops for a Christmas dinner, and we had a large pudding (stick-jaw) with currants and raisins, and we did not forget to drink the health of 'the auld folks at home,' in our tot of rum and water.*[25]

It is so bitterly cold, I can hardly hold my pen, and my feet are like ice, in spite of the beautiful boots which I received from home two days ago, the postage of which cost 32s; the flannel shirt has also come to hand. I wish I had thought sooner of asking mother to send me a few more things, but we did not expect to be encamped here so long; I want a large waterproof cape to go over the shoulders, and also a very large waterproof to go outside of one or two coats; some of the fellows have asked me to get half a dozen Shetland shirts, of a dark grey colour. If mother should send out another box, some pots of substantial preserved meats would be most acceptable; so much salt meat is very bad for one, and everything of that kind is an enormous price here.

Government is treating us very well in providing us with fur caps and sheepskin coats, and some underclothing. I see by the despatches that most of us are to have three medals; it has put the troops

[24] *My Early Soldiering Days*, printed at The Edinburgh Press in 1897.
[25] Captain Robert Nigel Fitzhardinge Kingscote, Scots Fusilier Guards, Lord Raglan's great-nephew and, through nepotism, one of the Commander-in-Chief's aides-de-camp.

in good spirits.[26] *I hope most of them will be spared to wear them at home; the poor soldiers have earned them dearly, and have had many discomforts. There is a proposal to make a railway from Balaclava to the siege train, which will be a great boon in aiding the transport.*[27]

On 18 June 1915 Major-General William Allan was one of just a dozen survivors to attend the 60th Anniversary Luncheon at the United Service Club.[28] He died on 12 July 1918 at Hillside, Bidborough, Kent.

[26] Governments were also parsimonious in Victorian times and most soldiers received just two: a British campaign medal with up to four bars (Alma, Balaklava, Inkermann [sic], Sebastopol) and one awarded by the Sultan of Turkey.

[27] The success of this project belies the popular view that all aspects of the Crimean War were dogged by poor administration: the thirty-nine mile railway was completed on 7 April 1855, little more than six weeks after Canada Works of Birkenhead had commenced work.

[28] Unsuccessful Anglo-French assaults on the Redan and the Malakoff, two of the lynchpins of the Fortress of Sebastopol, took place on 18 June 1855.

1855

Having narrowly escaped death during the battle of Inkerman, Captain George Frederick 'Fred' Dallas, 46th Regiment, was now aide-de-camp to Major-General Sir Robert Garrett, popularly known as 'General Chaos', who was commanding the 4th Division.[29] On 24 December 'Fred' Dallas wrote to his parents, Robert and Lucy, from 'Camp at Sebastopol':[30]

We have got up some Theatricals in our Division which are great fun, as there are some very good actors. The ladies have to be done by the tiniest of boys that now come out as Lieutenants and Captains, and it is great fun altogether. The Commander-in-Chief is coming tonight.[31] We have not room for many people, and there is immense trouble & interest to get a ticket, quite as much as to get Almacks in former days. I don't act myself but it is great fun. The most amusing part of the performance is 'getting up' the ladies. We cannot make them look even decently respectable. There is one boy in the 68th, with lots of light hair that is frizzled back and two little curls at the side à l'Impératrice, and ordinarily he is a very pretty, shy, modest-looking little boy, but when dressed up for his part, tho' in very quiet looking clothes, his appearance is anything but correct.[32] Another boy of ours has to act a very stout lady, and just as his turn came to go on the last night he came in great affliction to the manager to tell him, that 'his bosom was slipping gradually down to his knees'. However, he got on very well through his part, his bosom having been cunningly secured to his neck . . . I don't know of anything more to tell you or any question of yours to answer, so will wish you all a happy Xmas. We have a turkey tomorrow but he is I fear thin. We have two left, out of a flock, and have eaten all the family except these two, who have been fretting about the eaten ones I think, and over exert themselves. They are usually on the roof of our house, which can't be a good thing for them.

[29] More connections: the general and his ADC were not only in the same regiment, but they were also both educated at Harrow.
[30] *Eyewitness in the Crimea* edited by Michael Hargreave Mawson, published by Greenhill Books in 2001: reproduced with permission.
[31] Lieutenant-General Sir William Codrington, who was appointed on 11 November 1855.
[32] Lieutenant Francis de Luttrell Saunderson.

Having returned to England on 5 August 1856, Fred Dallas accompanied Sir Robert Garrett to China the following year, taking part in the action at Fatshan Creek on 1 June 1857 as a volunteer in the gunboat *Haughty*. In 1867 he married Maria Louisa, daughter of James Arthur Taylor MP, of Strensham Court, Worcestershire, retired by the sale of his commission in 1876, and died on 1 February 1888, aged fifty-eight.

1857/58

When the Indian Mutiny broke out, Lieutenant Henry Parlett Bishop was serving with 3 Troop, 3rd Brigade, Bengal Horse Artillery, stationed at Umballa, North-Western Provinces. On 12 May 1857 he wrote in his journal:

At 8 o'clock this morning heard that a despatch had been received by sunrise, by runner (telegraph wires having been cut) that serious disturbances had taken place, collision between sepoys and European Officers, in which several of the latter had been killed, Colonel Finnis, Capt. McDonald named, half the station had been burnt down, and part of the 3rd Light Cavalry had taken flight to Delhi.

He left Umballa on 27 May and was heavily engaged at the capture of Delhi that September. His column then marched on Lucknow, fighting much of the way, as he described in his journal that Christmas:[33]

24 December Thursday — We marched to Etah 18 miles, across a fine level country, with hard kutcha road, reaching our ground at 10 o'clock. At Etah, we found the Magistrate's and Collector's houses, and some others had been entirely destroyed but the school house strange to say was standing complete. Our force is the first that has visited Etah since the outbreak. We hear that Raja Tez Singh with 4 guns is at a place 16 miles from this so we are rather on the qui vive.

25 December Friday — Malour, marched at 5 o'clock and reached our ground a little after 10, Raja Tez Singh has retired to Mynpoorie of which he is Raja, and intends awaiting our arrival, he means fighting and no chaff. At least so we hear. At night the Engineers dined with us and we had a pleasant party till 10 o'clock when we broke up.

[33] Shelfmark MSS Eur C698: reproduced by permission of the Asia, Pacific and Africa Collections, The British Library.

Two days later Raja Tez Singh was comprehensively defeated at Mynpoorie: 'The results of the battle are eight guns of sorts taken, about 200 rebels killed, sixteen taken prisoner, and hanged, and occupation of the entire place – and all without a casualty on our side.' Lucknow was finally relieved in March 1858, after which 3 Troop was part of a column assisting in the reconquest of Oudh and the pursuit of Tantia Topi, one of the rebel leaders. Henry Bishop wrote in his journal:

25 December – Christmas Day – Took advantage of a rest at last to spend an idle day, for dinner we found ourselves on short commons, with nothing to drink but rum, and 2 bottles of sherry and 2 of beer I had.

Lieutenant Henry Bishop eventually returned to Umballa on 2 March 1859 and wrote: 'My house I found in very good order.' After a long and distinguished career, he retired from the Bengal Army as an honorary major-general and died in London on 14 January 1908, at the age of eighty.

1861

The American Civil War broke out on 12 April 1861, when Confederate forces attacked Fort Sumter, South Carolina. Lieutenant Alonzo Etheridge Bell, Confederate States Army, of Camden County, North Carolina was captured at Hatteras Inlet, North Carolina on 29 August 1861, when the first part of the Confederacy fell to Union forces. While imprisoned at Governor's Island, New York, he kept a diary, in which he wrote that Christmas:[34]

Weather cold. Snow upon the ground though not very deep. Ground frozen. It begins to look a little like Christmas. A great many packages were brought today: apples, raisins and eggs, cakes, etc. for to make a Christmas dinner for the men. But what difference in Christmas here and Christmas at home! For my part I feel very indifferent about the matter so far as eating is concerned. But suppose we had as well be merry as sad.

Another company arrived today. Long John Wentworth (as he is called) arrived here today on a visit to Col. Dimick. He is an abolitionist of the Greely manner & Philips school.

Night – Christmas Eve! How many tender memories come up the thought of Christmas Eve? How many little stockings will be hung up in the corners tonight for Santa Claus to fill. What sweet shew of toys, candys, etc. that old Santa Claus will bring for his favorites?

Christmas Day. And I would say a Merry Christmas to all! But who could say that when he was a prisoner in the hands of his enemies? Today thousands of religious devotees will assemble and chant forth pealing anthems and praises to the most high and yet the whole country is convulsed in the throws of a revolution in which brother is engaged against brother, father against son, friend against friend. What a strange anomaly is man? What an inconsistency?

The steamer brought a great many presents in the shape of turkeys, oyster cakes, etc. The generosity of kind friendly ladies to the prisoners. Christmas was kept up among the prisoners in

---

[34] Reprinted by kind permission of the North Carolina Office of Archives and History, Raleigh, North Carolina.

the same manner as at home. Many of our men actually got intoxicated. The officers were up early in the morning stirring eggnog.

Our boys have had a merry day of it. Singing, fiddling, sliding on the ice, etc., were resorted to — all seemed merry as a 'marriage bell.' The Yankees looked on in astonishment when he saw our table set for dinner. He had eaten but one piece bread during the day and he thought it strange he said that our fellows could have Lager enough to get drunk on when he could not even get a drink. They are very surprised at the feeling existing shown between our officers and men. They see there is a vast difference in our treatment of them and that of the Federals.

Our boys frequently talk with them and have a great deal of sport with them. We had a fine dinner. The bill of fare consisting of turkey, beef, butter, coffee, biscuits, mince pie, cakes, wine, etc. A great deal of this was sent us by a young lady of N. Jersey. We call her 'Little Jersey.'

The officers were so well pleased with the dinner that they gave 3 cheers for 'Little Jersey.' All seemed in high glee. But for the life of me I could not feel like Christmas. I was too, too, far from my loved ones.

1862

Private Taliaferro 'Tally' Simpson, 3rd South Carolina Volunteers, Confederate States Army, was born on 26 January 1839, the eldest son of South Carolina Congressman, Richard Franklin Simpson. On Christmas Day he wrote to his sister Anna from a 'Camp near Fredericksburg', where both sides had fought themselves to a standstill in December 1862:[35]

This is Christmas Day. The sun shines feebly through a thin cloud, the air is mild and pleasant, a gentle breeze is making music through the leaves of the lofty pines that stand near our bivouac. All is quiet and still, and that very stillness recalls some sad and painful thoughts. This day, one year ago, how many thousand families, gay and joyous, celebrating Merry Christmas, drinking health to absent members of their family, and sending upon the wings of love and affection long, deep, and sincere wishes for their safe return to the loving ones at home, but today are clad in the deepest mourning in memory to some lost and loved member of their circle. If all the dead (those killed since the war began) could be heaped in one pile and all the wounded be gathered together in one group, the pale faces of the dead and the groans of the wounded would send such a thrill of horror through the hearts of the originators of this war that their very souls would rack with such pain that they would prefer being dead and in torment than to stand before God with such terrible crimes blackening their characters. Add to this the cries and wailings of the mourners — mothers and fathers weeping for their sons, sisters for their brothers, wives for their husbands, and daughters for their fathers — how deep would be the convictions of their consciences?

Yet they do not seem to think of the affliction and distress they are scattering broadcast over the land. When will this war end? Will another Christmas roll around and find us all wintering in camp? Oh! That peace may soon be restored to our young but dearly beloved country and that we may all meet again in happiness. But enough of these sad thoughts. We went on picket in town

[35] *Far, Far From Home*, published by Oxford University Press: reproduced by permission of Oxford University Press, Inc.

a few days ago. The pickets of both armies occupy the same positions now as they did before the battle. Our regt was quartered in the market place while the others occupied stores and private houses. I have often read of sacked and pillaged towns in ancient history, but never, till I saw Fredericksburg, did I fully realize what one was. The houses, especially those on the river, are riddled with shell and ball. The stores have been broken open and deprived of every thing that was worth a shilling. Account books and notes and letters and papers both private and public were taken from their proper places and scattered over the streets and trampled under feet. Private property was ruined. Their soldiers would sleep in the mansions of the wealthy and use the articles and food in the house at their pleasure. Several houses were destroyed by fire. Such a wreck and ruin I never wish to see again . . .

While we were there, Brig Genl Patrick, U.S.A., with several of his aides-de-camp, came over under flag of truce. Papers were exchanged, and several of our men bought pipes, gloves, &c from the privates who rowed the boat across. They had plenty of liquor and laughed, drank, and conversed with our men as if they had been friends from boyhood.

'Tally' Simpson was 'shot through the heart whilst gallantly pushing forward in the front rank of his company' at Chickamauga on 20 September 1863.

1863

Major Thomas J. Key, Confederate States Army, of Phillips County, Arkansas, had transferred from the 15th Arkansas Infantry on 26 June 1862 and was now commanding Helena Artillery (Key's Battery). He wrote in his diary that Christmas:[36]

December 23rd — Since the cook had been sent out to purchase goods I did the cooking for the mess. He returned at night with a few articles which cost at the following rates: onions $2 per dozen; butter $3 per pound; chickens $3 each; pork $1 per pound; also some eggs at $3 per dozen to make some eggnog for Christmas. Today I wrote a lengthy letter to my wife, but the person I had intended to carry it had gone. This was a disappointment.

December 24th — This morning battalion guard mounting began for the three batteries. It is Christmas Eve. I am sitting in my little cabin and my thoughts carry me away to Helena where I see my good wife before the hearth with three children around her; the eldest a girl standing and looking earnestly into her mother's face; the second a boy five years old, sitting in a small chair looking into the fire; and the youngest a girl about four, leaning on her mother's lap — all listening attentively to what their intelligent mother is relating in regard to the visits of Santa Claus having visited them on former Christmas Eves with presents of toys, their curiosity is at its height to know if he will come tonight and fill their stockings. Ah, will not these little innocents be disappointed? Their father has not seen them for twenty months, and is now far away battling for home and liberty, and has no means by which he can convey them toys or money to purchase them. Whether their mother has the means to spare in procuring Christmas presents for them is unknown to me, but I pray heaven to provide her with the necessaries of life, and to bless and cheer the young and innocent hearts of my children during the Christmas holidays. Happy Christmas to my wife and children!

December 25th — Before breakfast the Doctor made some eggnog, a worthy luxury that is seldom

[36] *Two Soldiers: the Campaign Diaries of Thomas J. Key, C.S.A., and Robert J. Campbell, U.S.A.,* edited by Wirt Armistead Cate, published by the University of North Carolina Press in 1938: reprinted by kind permission of the University of North Carolina Press.

enjoyed in the army. Had sausages for breakfast, quite a treat, the first within the last twelve months. Ralph Bailey and Willie Smith called at my cabin about eleven o'clock, when Bailey made the second eggnog. All went smoothly in the battery. Out in the open air some of the men were hopping to the notes of an old fiddle, trying to be merry.

Thomas Key surrendered at Macon, Georgia on 20 April 1865 and took the oath of allegiance to the Union at Nashville, Tennessee on 11 May 1865.

1870

During the Franco-Prussian War Edwin Child, a twenty-four year-old Londoner apprenticed to Monsieur Louppe, a Parisian jeweller, was trapped in the city by the 'lignes Prussiennes'. He lived at 5 rue Scribe and joined 'the Garde Civique', which he describes as follows: 'corps formed for the keeping of the peace, half military, half municipal, arresting fugards, assisting firemen, superintending the closing of the Cafés, &c., &c. by this means we hope to employ ourselves usefully instead of sleeping'. On 23 November 1870 'after a joking kind of question from Mr. Louppe it being almost impossible to obtain any money from him, I volunteered into his company of *Garde Nationale de Marche*, i.e. into the 3rd Company of the 3rd Bataillon of which he is Sergeant Hourrier'. On Christmas Day Edwin Child wrote in his diary:[37]

Sunday 25th Up at ½ past 4, prepared our coffee & about 6 started for the outposts, this time without knapsacks, only our rugs & provisions: installed ourselves like moles in the underground 'huts', corvées for water & wood, aft^s card playing. 3 times on guard. 2 hrs day & 2 separate hrs at night. At 5 p.m. with 14 others volunteered to make a short reconnaissance in the village of Bagneux, which lay right in front of us, searched about 20 of the houses but without discovering the enemy, ret^d about 7 it blowing all the time a cutting wind that seemed to pierce you through & through. Captn and Lieut^t went with us and this is how I spent my Christmas, 1870. Could not prevent my thoughts reverting to those at home upon this day so sacred to all English hearts, especially while walking up & down upon guard & how often I said to myself What a Christmas! *as I pictured them all sitting down to a jolly good dinner, while I was without even a piece of steak or a decent soup to eat & feeling the blank my absence would cause, especially*

---

[37] Excerpts from the papers of Edwin Child published by kind permission of the Archives Collection, King's College, London.

under the circumstances they perhaps thinking me dead or nearly starved, were I at all delicate in my appetite the latter would not be far from the truth.

Sat 31st Up at 9. Appel at 11. Breakfasted with ami Bulfield, R. Molière and dined with Albert & Louise (his friend) at Tissot's Palais Royal, altho' the 103rd day of the siege we had 2 plates of meat (couldn't say of what) with sauces, & preserved green peas, found it remarkably good anyhow & relished it as such. Here, there & everywhere in aftn to keep blood in circulation. Freezing hard.

On 25 January 1871 Edwin Child resigned, 'feeling heartily disgusted with the whole affair', returned briefly to London, before getting caught up in the tragic events of the Paris Commune.[38] He lived later at Stockport, Lancashire and died in 1933.

[38] The Commune ruled Paris from 18 March to 28 May 1871, before being crushed by Maréchal MacMahon's government troops. Paris remained under martial law for the next five years.

1870

During the Siege of Paris the Horse-Eating Society tried to persuade the inhabitants not to disdain horsemeat. By Christmas even that source of supply was drying up and the animals from the Jardin d'Acclimatation in the Bois de Boulogne were duly offered to the highest bidder.[39] Alexandre Charon, the chef at the café Voisin, 261, rue St. Honoré, rose to the challenge and offered *des meilleurs morceaux* in his legendary menu for *le réveillon de Noël*:

Beurre, radis, sardines	Butter, radishes, sardines
Tête d'âne farcie	Stuffed ass's head
Purée de haricots rouge aux croûtons	Purée of red beans with croutons
Consommé d'éléphant[40]	Elephant soup
Goujons frits	Fried fish
Le chameau rôti à l'Anglaise	Roast camel, English style
Le civet de kangourou	Kangaroo stew
Côte d'ours rôties, sauce poivrade	Roast bear chops in pepper sauce
Cuissot de loup, sauce chevreuil	Haunch of wolf with venison sauce
Le chat flanqué de rats	Cat garnished with rats
Salade de cresson	Watercress salad
La terrine d'antilope aux truffes	Antelope and truffle terrine
Cèpes à la Bordelaise	Ceps, Bordeaux style
Petits pois aux Beurre	Buttered peas
Gâteau de riz au confiture	Rice pudding with jam
Fromage de Gruyère	Gruyère cheese

[39] Le Jardin d'Acclimatation was opened by Empereur Napoléon III on 6 October 1860.
[40] Sourced from *Castor* and *Pollux*, the pair of elephants that were formerly the pride of Paris.

The monkeys were spared because of 'exaggerated Darwinian instincts' that they were the relatives of the people of Paris and eating them would be tantamount to cannibalism while 'no butcher could afford the reserve price of 80,000 francs for the hippopotamus'.[41]

[41] *The Fall of Paris* by Alastair Horne, published by Macmillan in 1965.

1870

Crown Prince Frederick — only son and heir of Prussian Emperor Wilhelm I, husband of Prince Albert's and Queen Victoria's eldest daughter, Vicky, and father of Kaiser Wilhelm II — commanded the Third Prussian Army during the Franco-Prussian War. During the siege of Paris he and his staff spent Christmas in the Palace of Versailles:[42]

Headquarters: Versailles, 24th December — Christmas Eve, the great day when gifts of goodwill are distributed, in an enemy's country and in the midst of war's alarms! So this time we are not to spend this chiefest festivity of German family life with our dear ones. My heart is heavy indeed, yet for this year it seems that every feeling of kindly sentiment, nay, every instinct of humanity, must be overshadowed by the grimmest horrors of war. Next after my beloved ones at home, my thoughts are above all for the unhappy widows and orphans; for indeed for thousands this Christmas will be a time of mourning. God grant that when a year hence at the home fireside we recall the many sacrifices of this War, its results may at any rate be such that we can say with full conviction, they have been made to secure a lasting and honourable Peace! . . . For Christmas Eve I had organised a raffle under the Christmas tree for the eighty members of my Staff. The same was arranged in separate rooms for domestics, Staff guard, stable and escort squadrons; of course punch, pepper cakes, nuts and apples being provided as far as possible for the occasion. Every member of my Staff, as well as other invited guests, was bound each to bring with him two trifles for distribution, so that the caprice of fortune had a free scope; for instance Mr. Odo Russell won an officer's swordbelt.[43] The 160 prizes were soon disposed of amid much laughter and merriment, whilst I, to my surprise and delight, found a number of useful presents, thoughtfully chosen by wife

[42] *The War Diary of The Emperor Frederick III 1870–1871*, edited by A. R. Allinson, published by Stanley Paul & Co Ltd in 1927.

[43] Odo William Leopold Russell, later 1st Baron Ampthill, was attached to the German Army Headquarters on a special mission in November 1870. The following October he was appointed Ambassador in Berlin, where he spent the rest of his life, dying at Potsdam on 25 August 1884.

and mother, laid out on a table specially reserved for me. In particular, a miniature pocket-revolver met with much applause among the company; purses, pincushions, riding-satchels and other little toilet requisites were not wanting . . . Every guard-house was gay with Christmas trees and their glittering lights, which were to be found even at the most distant outposts. Everything wore quite the look of Christmas-tide at home, and a spirit of gay good humour enlivened every German heart even at points where the enemy's shells were whistling by.

Headquarters: Versailles, 25th December — Nine degrees of frost and an east wind as we went to service in the Palace chapel. It sounds like irony, amidst the miseries of war and in days that speak only of death and destruction to the foe to listen to the Christmas message of salvation: 'On earth peace and good-will toward men.' Christendom is still far from acting in the spirit of those words. The clergy have a difficult task set them to explain the contradiction involved in the strife of Christians against Christians, where each side invokes God for its own as the only just cause, and at every success holds this to prove that the adversary has been forsaken by Heaven . . . Skating is in active progress; for myself, I am not taking part in the amusement.

Just three weeks later, on 18 January 1871, the Crown Prince's father, Wilhelm, was declared Emperor (Kaiser) of Germany in the Hall of Mirrors at Versailles. Kaiser Frederick III ruled for only 99 days: having succeeded his ninety-one-year-old father, he died of throat cancer at Potsdam on 15 June 1888.

1878

During the Zulu War, Private Owen Ellis was a member of C Company, 1st Battalion, 24th Regiment. He wrote to his family at Caernarvon, North Wales from the Natal border on 31 December 1878:[44]

It is with pleasure that I write to you these few lines, hoping they will meet you all well and hearty, as I am at present, thank God. It is not necessary that I should tell you many words on this occasion,

[44] Letter published in *The North Wales Express*, 21 February 1879.

having written to you about nine days ago, but the reason that I do so early is that I have received three newspapers after sending you my last letter. The Genedl and the Penny Illustrated Paper were first received by me. On the 24th of this month the day before Christmas, viz. Tuesday, I was on guard from nine o'clock in the morning until nine o'clock on Christmas morning. About five o'clock on Tuesday afternoon, everybody were chatting about Christmas Day – some saying this and the others saying that, whilst others remarked how they would like to be spending their holidays at home. And there was I thinking how things were going on at home, portraying to myself how the boys were all together, and thinking a second time that I had told you that I would certainly be at home to make toffee. Well, across everything, about five o'clock, 'Owen Ellis' was called out in order to receive a letter from you, dated 20 November; and I was exceedingly glad to get it, and to learn that everybody was quite well. My mates were saying, 'I see, Ellis, you have had your Christmas Box already.' 'Yes', was my reply, and there I commenced to read the letter . . .

As I told you, I was on sentry duty on Christmas morning – and from one till three o'clock, and as I was parading backwards and forwards, I thought what a row there was at Caernarvon that night. There was not a sound to be heard around where I stood; the night was as dark as pitch and heavy rains descended from three till five o'clock in the morning. We afterwards enjoyed pleasant sunshine all day long; indeed, no one would believe that it had been raining. Well, I had Christmas Day all to myself; but there was no difference in the supply of food – we had only but what we got on ordinary days. Being many miles from any town or village, we did not expect anything else, and we were consequently obliged to be satisfied upon what we got. In Cape Town, things would have been quite different. I hope that you had a better treat than the one enjoyed on this occasion by me; but probably, if well and alive, I shall be at Caernarvon before next Christmas or somewhere about March or April, according to the manner in which the furloughs are issued from the orderly room. In this spot, Helpmakaar, the days are as fine as those of summer, but we meet every night with heavy rains, accompanied with thunder and lightning, which continue until six o'clock in the morning. On Saturday, 12 December, there fell a heavy shower of hailstones, which were as large as your fists, making it dangerous for anyone to be out at the time. Everybody was surprised at seeing such a thing. When the shower was over, pleasant sunshine appeared, and then everyone left their tents. You would have thought the white face of the earth was covered with mettling similar to that placed on the roads. One of the hailstones, weighed by the bandmaster, was three ounces in weight. I saw a hen that had been killed by the shower, all the feathers had been knocked off, and the body was bleeding frightfully. There is very good cattle pasture here, far better than what is on the other side, viz. Transkei, and this is beneficial to the farmers living in the surrounding locality . . .

The farmers who live in the surrounding country say that the Zulus will only be tempted to fight the Europeans once and that they will afterwards fly away for their lives, because they have not the weapons which we have . . . If well and alive, I shall let you know what will have taken place about the end of January. Well, it is time for me to conclude, but I must tell you that sports were held in our Regiment last Saturday — sports similar to those held 'Over the Aber', consisting of running, jumping, etc. You might thus think that to fight with Cetshwayo is but of little importance to the soldiers; indeed everybody thinks of returning home. I succeeded in getting some writing paper from a young Welshman named Davies. This is the last day of 1878, and I am happy to inform you that I and the boys are all in excellent health. Well, herewith I send my kindest regards a thousand times over.

Private Owen Ellis was killed at the Battle of Isandhlwana on 22 January 1879. On that terrible day, out of six companies of the 24th Regiment — a total of 21 officers and 581 non-commissioned officers and men — not one survived.

1885

Lieutenant Percy Wilfred Machell, 2nd Battalion, The Essex Regiment, fifth son of Canon Richard Beverley Machell, Lord of the Manor of Asby, Westmorland, and his wife Emma, sister of eighth Baron Middleton, was a member of the Gordon Relief Expedition, which reached Khartoum on 28 January 1885, two days after Major-General Charles 'Chinese' Gordon had been killed by the followers of the Mahdi. On 27 December 1885 he wrote to his father:[45]

We had a nasty accident about half way between Alexandria & Cairo. One of the Cameron Highlanders fell off the train trying to pass from one carriage to another, & when we got back to him we found his leg off, & a big hole in his head. The doctor had no amputating tools or chloroform with him, so he had to take off the jagged part with a table knife. The man was quite sensible, & made a good deal of noise. I should think there has not been such an operation for some years now. The doctor was a good performer, & we sent the man up to the citadel when we got to Cairo, but we heard since that he died a few hours after . . . I am getting good pay just now. 6/6 + 2/6 + 3/- + 3/- total 15/- a day & free living. It is not at all hot now, & the nights extremely cold. The weather to-day is about perfect. We expect to get to Kench to-night, Luxor next evening, & Assouan about six days from now. I expect we shall find the regiment gone on to Halfa at any rate. I keep very well, & can manage any work I have to do. I felt very disgusted at first about coming up again, but now I rather like it, & its advantages from a pecuniary point of view are undeniable. I spent my second Christmas day on the banks of the Nile, & it was more cheerful than the last when I was alone with one boat in the Dongola country. I & my captain gave the men a lot of beer that we bought at Sohag, & the servants turkeys, whisky & cigars. I think they enjoyed themselves very well, & behaved with more decency than soldiers generally do at Christmas. One of the 79th has a huge St. Bernard on board — it is such a pity as he is covered with sores already, & will be certain to die in a month or two. We manage to mess pretty well.

[45] Published by kind permission of the National Army Museum: NAM 2006–12–91.

The doctor is a very handy man & runs the business — we can buy any quantity of eggs, turkeys & chickens up as far as Assouan, but there the wilderness begins, & it is poor feeding after that to Halfa. You must get a good map now, Stanford, Charing Cross has the best, & you should get one on a large scale in order to make out small villages which become of tactical importance. Hope you are all right, & Sam.

Having spent most of his service in Egypt and the Sudan, Percy Machell took command of the 11th (Service) Battalion, The Border Regiment (Lonsdale) at Carlisle Racecourse on 25 September 1914.[46] After giving distinguished war service, for which he was awarded both the CMG and the DSO, he was killed at the head of his men during an attack on the Leipzig Salient, near Thiépval, on 1 July 1916, the first day of the Battle of the Somme. Almost two-thirds of his Battalion became casualties that day, including 23 of the 28 officers. Lieutenant-Colonel Percy Machell was fifty-three years old, a relatively advanced age for a battalion commander.

[46] Lord Lonsdale's provocative recruiting poster posed the questions: "Are You a Man or Are You a Mouse? Are you a man who will for ever be handed down to posterity as a Gallant Patriot, or Are you to be handed down to posterity as a Rotter and Coward?"

1899

On Christmas Day Lieutenant-Colonel Cecil Park, Devonshire Regiment, wrote to his wife, Caroline, from Ladysmith, Natal: [47]

All good wishes for you, and may God grant us a happier Christmas together next year. I hope someone nice has asked you to dinner to-night, so that you may not have a horrid solitary evening. I wish I could know that my last wire has reached you. It got through to Buller's force all right, but there is a little doubt whether it will be accepted and sent on without prepayment. It would be a cheerful little surprise for you after the long wait for news. The Boers began the morning by firing several shells, and we had to give up the early church parade, as the only place in which it can be held is just where the shells very often pitch. I stayed in bed till 5 a.m. for the first time in eight weeks, and got up by daylight, which was a great luxury. Then we had two eggs each for breakfast, so we feel quite festive already. I am going down to Communion at the English Church at eleven, then round the men's dinners at 12.30. There are some sports in the afternoon and a sing-song at night, and the men have an issue of rum, and tobacco, and their plum puddings, so they will not do badly. The carollers came round during the night, and sang rather well (in parts) the usual three hymns. I hear they visited Sir G. White and Colonel Knox, going round in one of the transport waggons.[48] The most extraordinary prices have been paid lately for foods and drinks in the garrison. A bottle of whiskey [sic] fetched £5 10s., and £5 is freely offered. Egyptian cigarettes, £5 a box. Eggs are 10s. 6d. a dozen, or 1s. each. We are getting a little fresh milk daily now at 2s. a bottle. £1 5s. was paid yesterday for fifty-two very small potatoes, and other things are in proportion. I fancy that after to-day's soufflé dehors there will be very few delicacies left in Ladysmith. I managed to collar a bottle of brandy yesterday and gave half to other fellows, and the rest I am keeping back in my flask for emergencies. I am wearing my colonel's badges to-day for the first time, and was grieved that I couldn't go on parade with them this morning. I also got my first note last night addressed to Lieut.-Colonel Park; it was from the

---

[47] *Letters from Ladysmith* by C. W. P., privately printed by W. Bishop.
[48] General Sir George White commanded the British troops besieged in Ladysmith.

Brigade Major, and gave me quite a jump when I first saw it. It takes off half the pleasure of it, not having you to enjoy it with me. I well remember how nice it was when the majority came in Rangoon, and how funny it seemed when everyone began addressing me as major. What a comfort it is to be absolved from the duty of trying to cultivate a major's figure! I can stay as thin as I like now to the end of the chapter. You had better get the name-board on the gate repainted before I come back, just to let people know a little.

On 6 January 1900 Cecil Park gallantly led the bayonet charge of three companies of his Regiment at Wagon Hill. The Boer attack was repulsed and three of the five officers present were killed, leaving just Park unwounded and Major James Masterson with a well-deserved VC. Major-General Cecil Park died on 29 March 1913, at the age of fifty-six.

1899

Stuart James Redpath trained at Guy's Hospital before emigrating to South Africa, where he practised as a pharmacist, initially in Johannesburg and later at Bloemfontein. On the outbreak of the Second Boer War he enlisted in the Ambulance Corps, Natal Mounted Rifles (Carabiniers) and was awarded the Distinguished Conduct Medal for his part in rescuing wounded men under fire at Caesar's Hill, Ladysmith on 6 January 1900.[49] Midway through the 118-day siege he wrote to his parents in West Norwood:

> Ladysmith Camp
> Natal Mounted Rifles
> December 28/29

Dear Mother and Father and all of you,

Just a few lines to let you know I am still alive and safe, but not in a very good condition of health. [three lines censored] I'm not very fat, you see. I spent a very rotten Christmas, and some pudding we tried to make made me ill next day. The heat in this hole is dreadful, and all the water has to be boiled; yet then there is a very large percentage of mud in it. I have had a lot of narrow escapes and hitherto have avoided fever. [two lines censored] Our hospital is full, and we had to erect a field hospital on some neutral ground. The place is above three miles from Ladysmith, so they are not shelled at all. Funny thing happened this morning. The Dutch shot a shell into the town, and it was picked up by someone, who found it contained plum pudding and the compliments of the season scratched on it.[50] Yesterday I had a clean wash, the first clean water I have had for

---

[49] The Boers sought the 'ground of tactical importance', a long, flat-topped hill overlooking Ladysmith: Caesar's Hill was at the east end of the ridge and Wagon Hill was at the west end — see the previous page.

[50] Fact is sometimes stranger than fiction!

two months. It was some rain water I got hold of. We are all very sick of the siege, and hope for relief, but it is a long time coming. If you are in communication with Willie, let him know where I am. Hoping you are well and safe. This letter is to be censored, so I must not tell you anything. Will write a longer letter with details when the line is open. Good-bye.

Your affectionate son,

Stuart J. Redpath

Stuart Redpath died in South Africa in 1961, aged eighty-five.

1899

Robert Joseph Cross was born on 26 August 1878, the son of Joseph Cross of 66 Aylestone Street, Leicester. He enlisted in the British Army on 15 February 1895, serving as a private soldier in the 1st Battalion, The Leicestershire Regiment throughout the Second Boer War. Having survived the Battle of Talana Hill on 20 October 1899 and the Battle of Lombard's Kop, which took place ten days later, Robert Cross was besieged at Ladysmith. On Christmas Day 1899 he wrote in his diary:[51]

Mon. 25th Xmas day and stuck in a small shelter four feet high we have been building walls all morning to make some new Kraals and have just knocked off our Xmas dinner which consists of Stewed Trek 1 tablespoonful of rum ½ oz. of Boer tobacco and a bit of what they call pudding made of Russian tallow which we use for greasing boots we only got a very small piece but it was too much for me. We are all talking of what we will do to make up for this when we get free and a Xmas in peace and the good things they will have. The last draft are telling what they were doing last year at this time and this is how Xmas day of 99 passed in the Seige [sic] but not without long toms compliments.[52]

At the end of the war Private Robert Cross was discharged from the British Army and, on 8 April 1903, he joined the County Borough of Leicester Police. He married Harriet Elizabeth Whitehouse on 4 April 1904 and retired from the Police on health grounds in May 1920. For ten years from 1932 he was the licensee of the *Lord Raglan* public house at 55 New Bridge Street, Leicester, dying there on 6 March 1942.

[51] *Military Miscellany II* – Army Records Society, edited by David Chandler with Christopher Scott, Marianne M. Gilchrist and Robin Jenkins, published in 2005: reprinted by kind permission of the Army Records Society.

[52] *Long Tom* was the nickname given to the three 8″ *Creusot* howitzers that the Boers sited on Pepworth Hill, four miles north of Ladysmith. In 1897 the Transvaal government had ordered these five-ton weapons from the French in order to protect Pretoria. The *Long Toms* could fire a 94lb projectile over six miles and one of them probably delivered the shell described by Stuart Redpath. The British Army responded in kind, using a pair of 6.3″ howitzers called *Castor* and *Pollux*.

1899

Colour-Sergeant James Taggart, Gordon Highlanders, who was also besieged in Ladysmith, wrote to his wife, Jane, in Aberdeen:[53]

A merry Christmas to you and our girlies and many happy returns of the day, happier I hope than the present one for you all and myself. You will remember one year ago we were fairly happy in Edinburgh. Today the Sergts had their Christmas dinner together in a large hole that has been dug out for the Quartermaster to issue rations from. The dinner was fairly good under the conditions, but not anything like what it would have been if we had been at home in Barracks. We had to sit on large biscuit boxes (wooden) and corned beef boxes & biscuit boxes made the table. It is the first time we have dined together since we landed in Natal, there is no Sergts Mess on active service.

I was on Picquet yesterday and we had to go out across the hill we were on to build a stone wall Sangar for a Camp they were going to make for the Brigadier. We got shelled by the Boer in the morning soon after we started, and when we went back after dinnertime they shelled us again from a hill called Telegraph Hill. They put three 100lb shells within a radius of 50 yards round us, but thank God no one was hit, although several men had narrow shaves. It was a very mad thing to do in broad daylight to send men out on top of a hill to work. The Boers kept up the shelling pretty briskly yesterday, they fired over 180 shells, but I don't think they did much injury. I have not heard of any body being hit. We had news on Christmas night that Kimberley was relieved and that the Boers had had heavy losses, also that General Buller hoped to have us relieved by New Years day, all of which I pray God may be true.

The Sergt Major has now rejoined us from Hospital but is not doing duty yet, as he cannot use his left hand. He said that most of our people in Intombi Hospl were doing well when he left, except that Morrison had a touch of fever and Sergt Marr a touch of dysentry. This disease is not abating any so far as I hear . . . We had a message from the Queen on Christmas day wishing us all well. These messages are all signalled from down country by the heliograph during the day and

---

[53] Letter quoted by kind permission of Ian Raffan Esq.

by lamp during the night. If the Boers would only attack us and come off the hills they are on around here, we would soon end the business for them here, but we are not strong enough to attack them in their positions, but as soon as the Relieving Column comes near enough to attack them we will likely help them. It will be a hard bloody fight but the Boers will have to go. I hear that 7000 militiamen have landed in Natal and that the Volunteers are doing Garrison duty at home. I wonder if the 3rd Battn are among them? I would like to meet some of the Permanent Staff out here.

James Taggart died of disease in Intombi Hospital on 9 January 1900. He was survived by his wife and their two young daughters, Mabel and Frances.

1910

George Edwin Howard Nettleton, born on 26 August 1885 in Bombay, was a bookbinder before enlisting in the Royal Marine Light Infantry on 6 July 1904. Having sailed from Chatham for China in HMS *Newcastle* on 29 September 1910, he wrote in his diary that Christmas:[54]

Xmas day 1910 Temp 90 shade. Divisions, etc. Archie & I made Xmas pudding. Pudding turned out a treat. Mess table had table cloth for once (a sheet we borrowed) & with Xmas cards etc we had each received & with the fruit etc to say nothing of photos of relatives & friends the mess looked quite homely. Usual section of dissatisfied ones with same old cry. What a Dam [sic] dry Xmas. Rum & lime juice not satisfying for Xmas. At 12 noon (5am London time) Capt & officers walked round mess deck & wished each mess a merry Xmas which was heartily returned & for one day social equality reigned & troubles forgotten. Festivities were kept up till pipe down at 10pm when every one returned to their hammocks with the thought that they had done their best to keep up a feast day which, wherever an Englishman & a U Jack are to be found, which will not be allowed to die out.

On 13 November 1916 George Nettleton was serving with the British Expeditionary Force in France and wrote in his diary that evening:

Attack started 5.45 A.M. . . . By 6.30 A.M. 5 of my crew knocked out. By 6.45 another two are gone. With only two men & myself left take the gun. Soon after I received a bullet in left thigh. Gave orders to other two men to get the gun back to H.Qtrs. I then got in shell hole and awaited dark. Enemy 15 yds away. About noon our artillery shelled enemy with shrapnel. Expected every moment to receive a present that was intended for Fritz. Excitement & loss of

[54] The papers of G. E. H. Nettleton in the Imperial War Museum Documents Collection: every effort has been made to trace copyright holders and the Imperial War Museum would be grateful for any information which might help to trace those whose identities or addresses are not currently known.

blood causes me to faint or lose consciousness which was a blessing. Dusk & I awake. Feel very weak but determined to try & crawl to dressing station. Stretcher bearers cannot come out because Fritz is firing at them as well as firing at the wounded. 2 stretcher bearers killed in trying their work of rescue. Reached our trenches safely & rolled in.

George Nettleton was later posted to 3rd Royal Marine Battalion, serving in the Aegean Islands. In late 1918 the Senior Medical Officer wrote: 'This N.C.O. was admitted to the R.N. Hospital, Mudros on Nov: 18th suffering from Influenza. From the commencement he was extremely ill. Temperature rising to 105F becoming more toxic daily and on Nov: 23rd at 23.00 death took place owing to heart failure. He was a splendid patient & most grateful for all that was done for him.' His wife, Daisy Alice, received a pension of 16s 3d a week, with an additional 6s 8d a week for their only child.

1914

Ten year-old Yves Congar lived with his parents in Sedan, the 'gateway' to France in both 1870 and 1940, which was occupied by the Germans just three weeks after the First World War began. By Christmas the Germans had adopted a policy of taking hostages on a daily basis. Yves wrote in his diary:[55]

It is Christmas Eve and we hope that next year will be better than the one we've just had. It is very cold, Dad is being held hostage overnight. There is no midnight mass. A year ago we'd walk in our clogs through the snow, and through the church's windows we could see a woman's hat bobbing along the old road. At the other end of the church lay our saviour — so many voices singing Christmas carols would rise to the sky!! Now foreign feet trample the old road and everything is silent and gloomy. It is because of the ruins that are still smoking, because of the burnt-out church and the menacing posters. It is the rule of the strongest; it is invasion and ruin; it is the cry of the hungry who don't even have a crust of bread; it is the resentment against the race that pilfers, burns and holds us prisoners; our country, which is no longer our home, when our cabbages, our leeks and all our other goods are in the hands of those thieves; the town is held to ransom, under oppression and the aggressor's injustice. Vengeance starts with a murmur, it's getting stronger and soon it will overflow like water in an already full cup, and in 10 years it will allow us to pay back the invaders with interest.

After the war Yves Congar became a Dominican priest and was one of the most important Catholic thinkers on ecumenism, the promotion of unity and cooperation between different religions. Having been actively discouraged by Pope Pius XII, he had a considerable influence on Pope John Paul II. Yves Congar was elevated to Cardinal in 1994 and died on 22 June 1995.

[55] From *A War in Words* edited by Svetlana Palmer and Sarah Wallis, published by Simon & Schuster in 2003: the editors expressed surprise that one so young could possibly have written like this and attributed it to a Mass that he had attended.

1914

From the camp of the Hood Battalion, 2nd Naval Brigade, Royal Naval Division at Blandford in Dorset, the poet Rupert Brooke wrote on Christmas Day to Cathleen Nesbitt:[56]

You give me a great many Christmas presents, don't you? I'm the unworthiest of recipients. And what can I send you from this camp? A wet stick, or a little boxful of mud. Those are the only alternatives — You know, the flask was the usefuller present: but the photograph was the nicer. It sits on a box by my bed, and brightens that rather gloomy hut. It's not much like you, *loveliest: but it is beautiful. One day you might get hold of a decent photographer, such as Schell or Oppé, and get them to take a proper photograph.*[57] *It could be done.*

I spend Christmas in looking after drunken stokers. One of them has been drunk since seven. He neither eats nor drinks, but dances a complicated step up and down his hut, half-dressed, singing 'How happy I am! How happy I am!' A short fat, inelegant man, in stockinged feet. What wonders we are!

He had clearly set the day aside for letter-writing, since he also found time to write to Noel Olivier:[58]

How old you must be! The Christmases fairly crowd past. And in what queer places I sing Adeste Fideles *in your honour! Last year Waikiki: this year the R.N.D.: next year beyond Acheron — I hope you're getting on well with — whatever you're getting on with: & that Margery's better & Daphne's still well.*[59] *Here it rains all day & every day. God be with you. Send me all the woollen things you weave —*

[56] *The Letters of Rupert Brooke* edited by Sir Geoffrey Keynes, published by Faber & Faber in 1968.
[57] The American Sherril Schell, who, in 1913, took the best-known photographs of Rupert Brooke.
[58] *Song of Love: The Letters of Rupert Brooke and Noel Olivier* edited by Pippa Harris, published by Bloomsbury in 1991: reproduced by kind permission of the publisher.
[59] Acheron — the underworld.

He was prophetic in referring to Acheron. The Royal Naval Division was sent to Gallipoli but Rupert Brooke contracted septicaemia, probably from a mosquito bite, and died in a hospital ship off the Greek island of Skyros on 23 April 1915. He was buried in an olive grove on Skyros, just two days before the Gallipoli landings.[60]

[60] Of the close friends in the burial party, only Arthur 'Oc' Asquith survived the war: Patrick Shaw-Stewart, Charles Lister and Denis Browne were all killed in action.

1914

Before he was conscripted Vasily Mishnin was a furniture salesman in Penza, central Russia. After two months of basic training, he left Penza railway station and his young, pregnant wife Nyura, on Christmas Day, bound for the trenches in Russian Poland. In his diary he wrote:[61]

The first bell — a shiver runs through my whole body. We take our places in the carriages. Pushing and shoving. Some are drunk, some sober. Everyone is clambering around the carriage. This doesn't feel like the right time to be saying goodbye, perhaps for ever.

The third whistle. Everyone breaks down. Loud crying, hysterics, whole families weeping. I kiss my Nyura for the last time and all of my family kiss me. I can hardly hold back the tears. I say goodbye to Nyura. She shouts, 'Why are you crying Vasiusha, you said you weren't going to cry!' Beside myself, I climb into the carriage with the rest and look out at the crown. I can hearing wailing, and a tumult of voices, but I've suddenly gone numb. My nerves are in shreds. I gaze at the pitiful crowd, but then my eyes find Nyura again and everything changes. I want to jump out of the carriage and kiss her again, for the last time. Too late, the long whistle of the steam train cries out, it's ready to separate us from our loved ones and take us — God knows where. I am about to climb out of the carriage, when something stirs under my feet. I feel the train moving. The crowd is whipped up into a yet more violent state of hysteria. My heart pounds as the carriage rolls on. We will perhaps never return to Penza.

We are pulled away from the doors and they are locked shut. Someone starts up our favourite tune, 'Today Must Be Our Final Day', to take our minds off all this, but I huddle up in a corner. The song upsets me so much, it is hard to compose myself. I feel ashamed. While my comrades sing, I can't stop crying, can't calm down.

Vasily Mishkin survived the war, returned to Penza, had three sons with Nyura and died in 1955, aged sixty-eight.

[61] From *A War in Words* edited by Svetlana Palmer and Sarah Wallis, published by Simon & Schuster in 2003.

1914

Josef Tomann, a young doctor from Eger in Hungary, was drafted into the Austro-Hungarian Army and sent to the city of Przemyśl to treat the sick and wounded in the garrison hospital. That Christmas, with the city invested by the Russian Army, Josef somehow found time to write in his diary:[62]

It is Christmas Eve and I'm here, on my own in a hostile country. I cannot rest today, my weary mind is troubled by dreams and sweet visions, that fill the air like phantoms. When we were children we looked forward to Christmas eve with great excitement. It was a time we always spent with our dear mother, but she will be on her own today crying over her three sons away at war.

Else was born this year. It was only last summer that Mitzl and I talked about how lovely it would be to have our first Christmas together. But we couldn't decide where to spend it. The war has made that decision for us. What is it like this year at home, I wonder? Do the lights on the tree twinkle as brightly? Sister Victoria showed me the Christmas tree, sprinkled with chalk and decorated with a few small candles. The poor chaps will be glad. I don't want to see or hear anything — I'll stay at home and try in vain to bury myself in a book. And yet twice I have felt hot tears on my cheeks. The war and its miseries have hardened me. Why am I so pathetic today? We cry every year, but this year we cry bitter tears.

On Christmas morning our scouts found three Christmas trees the Russians had left in no-man's land with notes that said something like: 'We wish you, the heroes of Przemyśl, a Merry Christmas and hope that we can come to a peaceful agreement as soon as possible.' There was a truce on Christmas Day, they neither attacked, nor fired.

On 22 March 1915 the surviving garrison of 110,000 finally surrendered to the Russians after a siege of 194 days. Exhausted by his experiences, Josef Tomann died on 16 May 1915, leaving Mitzl to bring up Else on her own.

[62] From *A War in Words* edited by Svetlana Palmer and Sarah Wallis, published by Simon & Schuster in 2003.

1914

At the outbreak of war Lieutenant-General Sir Douglas Haig was commanding I (British) Corps. On 24 December he wrote in his diary:[63]

At 11 am I presided over a meeting of GOC Divisions and CRA, CRE and General Gough to consider best method of carrying on operations under the new conditions. We discussed:

(1) a) *Trenches. [Size, depth and state, nature of revetment, etc.]*

   b) *Care of men. Not to be put into wet trenches up to their knees in water as has been done [in parts of this front.]*

(2) *Nature of Defence.*
    It must be active, otherwise enemy will advance and blow in our trenches with 'minen werfer' as he did to the Indians.

(3) *Trench Mortars. Personnel to be gunners or specialists.*

(4) *Hand Grenades. Keep enemy at a distance as long as possible. Use outposts entrenched.*

(5) *Local Attack. As in the old days*
    Bomb throwers
    Bayonet party
    Attacking body, with flank detachments etc.

(6) *General Attack. I asked GOCs to get to know the ground so as to be ready for a general advance when the time comes . . .*

Tomorrow being Xmas day, I ordered no reliefs to be carried out, and troops be given as easy a time as possible.

Alan Fletcher, Straker and Secrett[64] [helped me to tie up and address my] *Xmas*

---

[63] *War Diaries and Letters 1914–18* edited by Gary Sheffield and John Bourne, published by Weidenfeld & Nicolson in 2005. (© 2005 the estate of Earl Haig and the editors): reproduced by permission of Peters Fraser & Dunlop Group Ltd.
[64] Haig's ADCs and his soldier-servant.

parcels. Doris sent [me a nice present] *for everyone on my Staff: some 36* [in all, including the] *servants. And Leo Rothschild sent me 50 odd pairs of fur-lined gloves! All sent out with a line 'Best Wishes for Xmas from Lady Haig', or from Leo Rothschild, as the case may be. This kept me employed till past midnight. But what an amount of pleasure it gave me to distribute Doris' Xmas gifts in the midst of all my anxiety!*

On Boxing Day Sir Douglas Haig took command of the newly-created British First Army.

1914

Perhaps the most famous wartime Christmas incident is the Truce of 1914. The account given by Captain Sir Edward Hulse, Bt, 2nd Battalion, Scots Guards is one of the best-known:[65]

At 8.30 a.m. I was looking out, and saw four Germans leave their trenches and come towards us; I told two of my men to go and meet them, unarmed *(as the Germans were unarmed), and to see that they did not pass the half-way line. We were 350—400 yards apart at this point. My fellows were not very keen, not knowing what was up, so I went out alone, and met Barry, one of our ensigns, also coming out from another part of the line. By the time we got to them, they were three quarters of the way over, and much too near our barbed wire, so I moved them back. They were three private soldiers and a stretcher-bearer, and their spokesman started off by saying that he thought it only right to come over and wish us a happy Christmas, and trusted us implicitly to keep the truce. He came from Suffolk, where he had left his best girl and a 3½ h.p. motor-bike! He told me that he could not get a letter to the girl, and wanted to send one through me. I made him write out a post card in front of me, in English, and I sent it off that night. We then entered into a discussion on every sort of thing. I was dressed in an old stocking-cap and a man's overcoat, and they took me for a corporal, a thing which I did not discourage, as I had an eye to going as near their lines as possible. I asked them what orders they had from their officers as to coming over to us, and they said none; they had just come over out of goodwill . . .*

I kept it up for half an hour, and then escorted them back as far as their barbed wire, having a jolly good look round all the time, and picking up various little bits of information which I had not had an opportunity of doing under fire! I left instructions with them that if any of them came out later they must not come over the half-way line, and appointed a ditch as the meeting place. We parted after an exchange of Albany cigarettes and German cigars, and I went straight to H.-qrs. to report. On my return at 10 a.m. I was surprised to hear a hell of a din going on, and not a single

[65] *Letters Written from the English Front in France between September 1914 and March 1915*, privately printed in 1916.

man left in my trenches; they were completely denuded (against my orders), and nothing lived! I heard strains of 'Tipperary' floating down the breeze, swiftly followed by a tremendous burst of 'Deutschland über Alles', and as I got to my own Coy. H.-qrs. dug-out, I saw, to my amazement, not only a crowd of about 150 British and Germans at the half-way house which I had appointed opposite my lines, but six or seven such crowds, all the way down our lines, extending towards the 8th Division on our right . . .

Meanwhile Scots and Huns were fraternising in the most genuine possible manner. Every sort of souvenir was exchanged, addresses given and received, photos of families shown, etc. One of our fellows offered a German a cigarette; the German said, 'Virginian?' Our fellow said, 'Aye, straight-cut': the German said, 'No thanks, I only smoke Turkish!' (Sort of 10/- a 100 me!) It gave us all a good laugh.

A German N.C.O. with the Iron Cross — gained, he told me, for conspicuous skill in sniping — started his fellows off on some marching tune. When they had done I set the note for 'The Boys of Bonnie Scotland, where the heather and the bluebells grow', and so we went on, singing everything from 'Good King Wenceslaus' down to the ordinary Tommies' song, and ended up with 'Auld Lang Syne', which we all, English, Scots, Irish, Prussians, Wurtembergers [sic], etc.,

joined in. It was absolutely astounding, and if I had seen it on a cinematograph film I should have sworn that it was faked!

Captain Sir Edward Hulse, who was unmarried, was killed in action at the battle of Neuve Chapelle on 12 March 1915, at the age of twenty-five. He was succeeded in the baronetcy by his uncle.

1914

In the German princely tradition Crown Prince Wilhelm of Prussia, the eldest of five sons of Kaiser Wilhelm II and a grandson of Queen Victoria, took command of the 5th German Army in August 1914.[66] In his war memoirs he wrote of that Christmas Eve in the Argonne:[67]

I spent the afternoon in the hutments of the Württembergers with the 120th and 124th Regiments. Thick snow lay on the hilltops above this Forest of the Dead. The shells howled their monotonous and hideous melody, and from time to time the sacred silence was rent by the burst of a machine-gun's fire. And in between, one could hear the dull drone of the trench mortar shells. Nevertheless, the spirits of the men were everywhere very cheerful. Every dugout had its Christmas tree, and from all directions came the sound of rough men's voices singing our exquisite old Christmas songs.

Kirchhoff, the concert singer, who was attached to our Headquarters Staff for a while as orderly officer, sang his Christmas songs on that same sacred evening in the front-line trenches of the 130th Regiment.[68] And on the following day he told me that some French soldiers who had climbed up their parapet had continued to applaud, until at last he gave them an encore. Thus, amid the bitter realities of trench warfare, with all its squalor, a Christmas song had worked a miracle and thrown up a bridge from man to man.

After his early successes in the Argonne, Wilhelm was made responsible for the German offensive against Verdun, which began on 21

---

[66] The British took no such chances: Edward, Prince of Wales, was a staff officer – kept away from the front line – in France, Egypt and Italy during the First World War although his brother, Prince Albert (later HM King George VI), did see action in HMS *Collingwood* at the Battle of Jutland.

[67] *My War Experience*, published by Hurst & Blackett in 1922. At the same time Crown Prince Rupprecht, heir to the throne of Bavaria, was commanding the 6th German Army in Lorraine.

[68] Walter Kirchhoff was renowned as a Wagnerian singer. Of his role as Walter von Stolzing in a 1913 Covent Garden production of *Die Meistersinger von Nürnburg*, *The Times* reviewer wrote: 'Mr. Kirchhoff gives what one so rarely gets in a Wagnerian tenor, a combination of vocal power and manly personality, which is essential to a satisfactory representation.'

February 1916. That September he was promoted to lead Army Group Crown Prince but the following year, disillusioned with the progress and conduct of the war, he tried — unsuccessfully — to persuade Chancellor Bethmann-Hollweg to sue for peace. In May 1918 his armies enjoyed some success during Operation *Blücher-Yorck* on the Aisne, before the German collapse of late 1918. On 12 November 1918 he signed the abdication document and later went into exile at Doorn in Holland. He was eventually allowed to return home and died at Hechingen in Baden-Württemberg, the ancestral home of the Hohenzollern dynasty, on 20 July 1951.

1914

Before the war Albert Downes of Twelve Houses, Hafodyrynys, whose father had served in the Army for 12 years, was employed as a miner at Llanhilleth Colliery. In 1912 Albert Downes joined the Territorials, without his parent's knowledge. Soon after the outbreak of war he was serving with 2nd Battalion, The Monmouthshire Regiment in France and wrote home from there:

28th December 1914

Dear Mother,

I now write these few lines to let you know that I am allright, and to thank you for the parcel I received safe on Boxing Day. We were in the trenches on Christmas Day and we came out in the evening. We had a very merry Christmas considering the difficulties we are in at the present. The Germans were very merry, and they were singing all night and we gave them a few songs in return. We had plenty of presents sent to us for Christmas. I dare say you have seen a few letters in the Free Press.[69] I hope you will have a very prosperous New Year. I had a letter from Enoch Roberts about his brother's death, but we are not allowed to say anything about it. Hoping you and the family are allright.

Your Loving Son,

A. Downes.

P.S. I have come across Llew Davies and Bryn Gibb. They had Christmas Day in the trenches with us, and I gave them a share of my parcel, as they are attached to a different Company.

---

[69] *The Free Press of Monmouthshire.*

1914

Captain Reginald Hobbs served with Albert Downes in 2nd Battalion, The Monmouthshire Regiment. On Christmas Day he wrote to his wife, Cissie, from a fanciful, but no doubt accurate, address:[70]

Little Grey Home
Watery Lane
Xmasday 1914

My own darling girl,

Had your two letters and two letter cards posted from Sydney this morning and was glad to get them, well old girl here we are Xmas day in the trenches of course it's rather difficult to realise that it is Christmas except that we had an order over the 'phone this morning that no firing was to take place at all unless absolutely necessary & now there is hardly a shot fired by them and it sounds almost peaceful. My fellows have been singing carols & so have the Germans however I've just warned my Sentries to be extra on the look out because I don't trust 'em a yard. What say you? I've had a fireplace dug in the trench wall opposite my hut & have a blazing log fire going. Our fellows got the logs last night a perilous job but worth it and so I've been sitting down and gazing into the flames thinking of you and my people at home & picturing your doings as far as I can. We are being relieved this evening & are going to keep Xmas properly as far as we can in Billets . . . I meant to have finished this and posted it Xmas Day but I was stopped by being informed that about 100 Germans had got out of their trenches in front of my company I suppose they knew we wouldn't fire at them and were burying their dead. There are heaps about half way between — of course I thought they must be up to some game, digging new trenches or something so I sent a few of my fellows out to see — they walked up to the groups shook hands & chatted in a most friendly way for quite an hour. Of course none of the men who were out had any arms or should

---

[70] Published by kind permission of Mrs Sandy Walford.

have fired at them. Quite a lot of their men could talk English well & said they were all pretty fed up & hoped the war would soon be over – they exchanged cigarettes & souvenirs &c & then they all went back & so did our chaps. It was a most peculiar sight I can assure [you] & I don't expect you will believe me but it is an honest fact Cissie.

Reginald Hobbs was absolutely right to be cautious: on the last day of the year Albert Downes died from gunshot wounds to the head. Despite being wounded twice later in the war, and also being gassed, Reginald Hobbs survived to become land agent to the Duke of Beaufort. He died on 10 September 1971.

1914

The British hoped to use the cover of the holiday season to neutralise the Zeppelin threat. Commander Hugh Miller was Paymaster on board the light cruiser HMS *Arethusa*:[71]

During December Seaplane Carriers were attached to our squadron and one or two abortive attempts had been made to attack the Zeppelin sheds at Cuxhaven. On Christmas Eve, however, we left Harwich on another attempt. In company with Arethusa *were* Undaunted, Fearless *and the Harwich Force destroyers and also the* Engadine, Riviera *and* Empress *carrying nine seaplanes. The* Fearless *and her destroyers were despatched to make a demonstration off Emden, but the remainder of us continued steaming towards Heligoland. It was a dark night and as I prepared to take up my lonely vigil in the After Control Position I was told that it was obvious the enemy knew we were in their waters as we had passed through a fleet of fishing trawlers and some had evidently been fitted with W/T. Our operators had heard a good deal of low powered wireless followed very soon by liveliness on many high powered German stations which, we presumed, were issuing warnings and operational orders. The development of the photograph promised therefore to be interesting. As the cold light of dawn approached the two nearer destroyers following on either beam astern of us became mysterious dark objects of uncertain size. Surely, I remember thinking, they were too large for destroyers. Soon it was obvious we were near Heligoland and our speed was reduced as if to make our approach more silent. Minute by minute the light grew stronger and one by one our little squadron appeared out of the darkness. I searched the horizon for any signs of the enemy. Suddenly we stopped and in the early morning light I could see the seaplane carriers hoisting out their machines. By the time this was done it was quite light and ahead of us Heligoland was easily visible with a church spire sticking up in the centre of the Island. The seaplanes at once began to test their engines and buzzed about amongst the ships making a tremendous din. They looked like so many flies trying to disentangle themselves from sticky paper: none apparently could*

---

[71] The papers of Rear-Admiral H. Miller CB DSO in the Imperial War Museum Documents Collection: by kind permission of his niece, Patricia Miller.

get off the sea, and then away to the northward a mysterious bank of smoke appeared and we realised the enemy ships were near at hand. Still the seaplanes seemed stuck and over Heligoland a Zeppelin rose in the air and pointed towards us. I thought that if one of our objects was to entice the enemy to sea we were fairly sure of success this time. At last a seaplane rose into the air and then another and another and away they headed for the enemy coast. Two, however, would not rise and at length orders were given to hoist them inboard. More delay. At last this was done and away we headed at 15 knots for the rendez-vous where we were to pick up the aeroplanes on their return. The Zeppelin followed us and soon we saw a plane flying towards us from astern. At first we thought it was one of our own machines returning, but she turned out to be a 'Hun'. We had no anti-aircraft guns and so the Commodore ordered rifles to be served out to the stokers off watch so that they could engage the enemy. Personally I thought the stokers would be more dangerous than the 'Hun' who passed over us at not more than 1,000 feet from our deck. He dropped his bombs on either side of us but he looked so harmless that I felt like waving to him and telling him to run off home. It was a lovely Christmas morning and quite warm with a smooth and sparkling sea. We felt that this kind of warfare was rather good fun.

Rear-Admiral Hugh Miller died on 21 August 1972.

1914

Having lost both his parents during the Boxer Rebellion, Thomas Benjamin Dixon was educated at the School for the Sons of Missionaries, Lewisham, before training as a doctor at University College Hospital, London. Commissioned as a Surgeon, RNVR, he soon found himself in the South Atlantic in the cruiser HMS *Kent*. On 8 December 1914 the British Squadron had destroyed four out of five of Admiral Graf Maximilian von Spee's cruisers at the Battle of the Falklands. In his diary Thomas Dixon describes Christmas, which was spent at ValleNar roads, Chile:[72]

Christmas Day. Yesterday after coaling some of us tried to get ashore to get holly for decorations. A squall was blowing and although the officers double-banked the oars with the crew of the lifeboat we could make no headway against the wind and tide and ignominiously drifted to leeward. We were seen and rescued by the Glasgow's *steam boat which towed us back. Later on in the afternoon the C.P.O.s got there in calmer weather and brought back a boat load of arbutus, laurel, berberis, wild fuchsia trees and plenty of flowers, lilies, fuchsias and unknowns. So this morning we had a fuchsia tree at the top of each mast. Its red flowers made it look just like holly. The crew borrowed some of the officers' clothing and made up to represent us. They held a mock court martial which was great fun and imitated us beautifully. At 12 the Captain visited all the messes followed by the officers who had to taste the various plum puddings and other goodies. It was amazing to see what there was still in the ship in the way of extra food and how cheerful the men were in spite of no beer. In the ward room we had asked the warrant officers and the midshipmen to join us in some champagne before lunch. While there, a parcel arrived from 'the Mayor of Margate' for Dunn. It contained a set of infant's underclothing — Dunn being a bachelor. We hung the articles along the light rail above the table and they made an interesting decoration. The clothes arrived amongst the other things sent by the ladies of Kent apparently. After lunch the*

[72] *The Enemy Fought Splendidly*, published by Blandford Press in 1983: reprinted by permission of Cassell Plc, a division of The Orion Publishing Group (London).

crew seized on every officer and carried him round the decks behind the funny party and a 'band'. Some officers went ashore in the afternoon. The P.M.O. being ill in bed with dysentery I stayed aboard. Very hard luck on Fleet Surgeon being ill at such a time. We did our best to cheer him up, however. After the return of the shore party laden with huge tree ferns, fuchsias, etc., we had a sing-song and some excellent new songs, one of which had escaped the lynx-eyed censor (the parson) and was much enjoyed, or at least two verses of it, 'Little by little, and bit by bit.' Our dinner in the evening was a triumph for the Paymaster and the Cook. The decorations of ferns, fuchsias and lilies and baby's garments were really beautiful. Turtle soup. Pate de foie gras, turkey and salmon cutlets, and plenty of fizz and plum pudding. Afterwards the fun was kept up well. Jones' song, and Burn's dancing being the features, especially the latter's last effort in an impromptu Salome costume. The Captain was our guest for the evening. We all remarked that it was the cheeriest Christmas on a ship we could remember and felt sorry for the sad folk (probably) at home.

Thomas Dixon was later appointed Honorary Physician to HM King George VI and received the CBE for his services during the Second World War. He died on 16 March 1960, at the age of seventy-three.

1915

Lieutenant Edwin Evan Jones, Royal Army Medical Corps, sailed for Mesopotamia on 21 December 1915 in SS *Vita*. Four days out of Marseilles, they stopped at Malta, as Edwin Jones described in his diary:[73]

'A Happy Christmas to all.'

Taken into Valetta [sic] *Harbour 7 a.m., a sight that I shall never forget. The sun was just rising and the lovely rocks standing out, dotted with huge buildings. A quantity of small boats came alongside, and small native boys doing all kinds of tricks in the water. Most of the officers were ashore by 10 a.m., but we were not allowed.*

I have had some very rough meals on active service, but getting bully beef and biscuits on Christmas Day beats all. We all wished to be back in France; the food we were getting was terrible. At 2.30 p.m. I was granted a pass to go ashore with three other men. We hired a small boat alongside, and he took us ashore, but, of course, we didn't leave him on friendly terms, but of course, Tommies are always generous.

It seemed to be up, up, up, goodness only knows why they built so many steps, but when we got to the top, it was a glorious sight. We raided a shop for picture postcards and other kinds of presents to send home. We made some bargains with fruit, at least, we thought so, but am afraid, after all, we were done. After sight-seeing and our time nearly up (we only had 2½ hours) we met an English Tommy who insisted on us going back to his station to drink the health of Christmas Day.

And we did so freely. I counted about 150 steps going up, but only about 50 coming down, and Sergeant Ash swore there were, at least, 7 or 8 hundred. Oh, dear, no! It wasn't the whiskey, but 'Sun', as you must remember we had been through the greater part of the winter in France. What a rush to get back to the boat! What with baskets of fruit, &c., and our heads all of a whirl, we

---

[73] *War Reminiscences: France, Egypt, Mesopotamia 1914–16* by E. E. Jones, which was privately printed: reprinted by kind permission of Dr Robert Griffith Jones.

managed it safe. Concert at night, and all our superior officers well away, while poor Tommy had none. To bed, all disheartened at the hardship of the day.

Edwin Jones served with the forces attempting to relieve Kut, was evacuated to Egypt in June 1916 but, instead of going to 'Blighty', as he had hoped, he joined Allenby's army, eventually advancing as far as Damascus. Still wearing his lightweight, tropical uniform, Edwin Jones caught pneumonia on the troopship returning to England and died at Aberdovey on 25 September 1919.

1915

Captain (later Colonel) Richard Meinertzhagen – big-game hunter, colonial officer, ornithologist, prolific author and dedicated Zionist – served as an intelligence officer in German East Africa during what William Boyd described as *An Ice-Cream War*.[74] Back at Karunga, Victoria Nyanza, he wrote in his diary of his Christmas Day experiences:[75]

At 5 p.m. we located four tents, fires burning and, by the mercy of God, no precautions, no sentries, and men lounging about. The country was good for stalking and we were well in position for a rush at dusk. In fact, the men having left their rifles in their tents and there being no sentry, we rushed them silently from not more than a few paces. We used bayonets only and I think we each got our man. Drought got three, a great effort.[76] I rushed into the officers' tent, where I found a stout German on a camp bed. On a table was a most excellent Xmas dinner. I covered him with my rifle and shouted to him to hold his hands up. He at once groped under his pillow and I had to shoot, killing him at once. My shot was the only one fired.

We now found we had seven unwounded prisoners, two wounded and fifteen killed, a great haul. I at once tied up the prisoners whilst Drought did what he could for the wounded. We covered the dead with bushes and I placed sentries round the camp and sent out a patrol of three men. Drought said he was hungry, so was I, and why waste that good dinner? So we set to and had one of the best though most gruesome dinners I have ever had, including an excellent Xmas pudding. The fat German in bed did not disturb us in the least, nor restrain our appetites. After that excellent meal, I searched the German's kit: I have shot a Duke, the first Duke I have killed.[77] His luncheon basket was a most elaborate arrangement, with plated dishes and cutlery, all marked with a coronet. These Drought and I purloined, thinking it a pity to leave them to be looted by the natives.

[74] *An Ice-Cream War* was published in 1982.

[75] *Army Diary 1899–1926*, published by Oliver & Boyd in 1960: reproduced by kind permission of the Estate of Colonel Richard Meinertzhagen CBE DSO.

[76] Captain James J. Drought, who commanded the 'Skin Corps', a frontier unit of Ugandan askari scouts.

[77] In the original transcript the Duke was identified as Graf Wecklenburg.

We cleared out after dark, but were unable to bury the bodies, having no tools with which to dig.
With our prisoners we marched till midnight and then slept with sentries out and were off again
on the 26th and reached here without incident yesterday afternoon.

The following year Richard Meinertzhagen was awarded the DSO for his role in the East African campaign. He then joined the Egyptian Expeditionary Force and met T. E. Lawrence.[78] Towards the end of the war he went to the Western Front and later took part in the Peace Conference at Versailles. In 1957 Richard Meinertzhagen was awarded the CBE for services to ornithology. He died on 17 June 1967, at the age of eighty-nine.

[78] In *Seven Pillars of Wisdom*, Lawrence wrote: 'This ally was Meinertzhagen, a student of migrating birds drifted into soldiering, whose hot immoral hatred of the enemy expressed itself as readily in trickery as in violence . . . Meinertzhagen knew no half measures. He was logical, an idealist of the deepest, and so possessed by his convictions that he was willing to harness evil to the chariot of good. He was a strategist, a geographer, and a silent laughing masterful man; who took as blithe a pleasure in deceiving his enemy (or his friend) by some unscrupulous jest, as in spattering the brains of a cornered mob of Germans one by one with his African knob-kerri. His instincts were abetted by an immensely powerful body and a savage brain, which chose the best way to its purpose, unhampered by doubt or habit.'

1915

George Coppard, nephew of the short-story writer A. E. Coppard, was born on 26 January 1898 and left school at the age of thirteen to work for a firm of taxidermists. In August 1914 he enlisted in the Queen's Royal West Surrey Regiment, even though he was under-age. After training at Guildford, he was posted to France, just in time to take part in the Battle of Loos. That December he moved into the front line at Festubert with the Machine-gun Section of the 6th Battalion of his Regiment:[79]

It was Christmas Eve, and just after dark a second lieutenant came to visit us. I think his name was Clark. Among other things, he came to remind us that by order of the Commander-in-Chief there was not to be any fraternising with the enemy on Christmas Day.[80] The whole world knew that on Christmas Day, 1914, there was some fraternising at one part of the line, and even an attempt at a game of football. Troops in the front line a year later were naturally speculating on whether a repeat performance would develop and, if so, where. Speaking for my companions and myself, I can categorically state that we were in no mood for any joviality with Jerry. In fact, after what we had been through since Loos, we hated his bloody guts. Our greatest wish was to be granted an enemy target worthy of our Vickers gun.

Sad it is for me to tell that Mr Clark was shot through the head shortly after arriving on the island. A machine gun swept the breastwork and got him. He died on the little strip of earth in the early hours of Christmas Day. It seemed to be another case of a life thrown away because a man was tall. Mr Clark was a giant. I can't understand how the military bosses overlooked the shocking handicap which tall men were under in trench warfare. It will never be known how many men lost their lives from wounds received at the six foot mark or above. Surely the artillery was the place

[79] *With a Machine Gun to Cambrai*, published by HMSO in 1969: reproduced under the terms of PSI licence number C2007001361.
[80] General Sir Douglas Haig had assumed the appointment of Commander-in-Chief of British Forces in France and Flanders on 19 December 1915.

for tall chaps, where they were not over-vulnerable by reason of their height. It was bad enough for me at five feet nine and a half to have to keep remembering the height of the parapet. Our thoughts turned to home and our loved ones on Christmas Day. No letters came; no parcels; nothing. The soggy rations were of the meanest kind, the only pretence at Christmas being a few raisins covered with hairs and other foreign matter from the inside of a sandbag. Stretcher-bearers came after dark for the dead young officer. They had a terrible job carrying him over the duckboards.

In November 1917 George Coppard was seriously wounded at the Battle of Cambrai and was later awarded the Military Medal. After the war he worked as a waterguard officer at HM Customs and Excise and later as an Executive Officer at the Ministry of National Insurance. He died on 17 February 1985.

1915

Wounded in the thigh the previous year by a ricochet from his drawn sword — treated by the application of cow patties — Major Sir Iain Colquhoun, Bt, Scots Guards, was now in the Neuve Chapelle sector:[81]

December 25th Xmas Day — Stood to at 6.30. Germans very quiet. Remained in Firing trenches till 8.30 am. No sign of anything unusual. When having breakfast around 9 am a sentry reported to me that the Germans were standing up on their parapets, and walking towards our barbed-wire. I ran out to our Firing trenches and saw our men looking over the parapet, and the Germans outside our barbed-wire. A German officer came forward and asked me for a truce for Xmas. I replied that this was impossible. He then asked for ¾ hr. to bury his dead. I agreed. The Germans then started burying their dead and we did the same. This was finished in ½ hrs. time. Our men and the Germans then talked and exchanged cigars, cigarettes etc. for ¼ of an hour, and when the time was up, I blew a whistle, and both sides returned to their trenches. For the rest of the day the Germans walked about and sat on their parapets. Our men did much the same but remained in their trenches. Not a shot was fired. At night the Germans put up Fairy lights on their parapets, and their trenches were outlined for miles on either side. It was a mild looking night with clouds, and a full moon and the prettiest sight I have ever seen. Our machine guns played on them, and the lights were removed. Our guns shelled heavily all night at intervals of ½ an hour, and the Germans retaliated on Sunken Road. I had to leave my dug-out five times during the night owing to shells.

26th December — The Brigadier (who came round my trenches 10 mins. after my truce was over) doesn't mind a bit, but the Major-General (Cavan) is furious about it.

30th December — The row about the Xmas truce is still going on. I had to write my account of the thing about 8 times.

4th January — At 8.30 received note from the Colonel telling me that I was under close arrest for my share in the Xmas Day truce.

[81] The papers of Lieutenant-Colonel Sir Iain Colquhoun Bt DSO in the Imperial War Museum Documents Collection: by kind permission of Malcolm Colquhoun.

17th January — I am accused of conduct to the prejudice of good order & military discipline in
that on the 25th Dec I (1) agreed to a truce with the enemy (2) permitted a cessation of hostilities.

Three days later the result comes out. The sentence which is 'Reprimanded' has been quashed
by G.H.Q. but the conviction remains which really means that the whole thing is washed out. The
whole Guards Division and anyone who knows the facts of the case all say it was a monstrous thing
that the Court Martial ever took place.

The Court Martial did not have an adverse effect on Sir Iain
Colquhoun's subsequent career. He was promoted to lieutenant-
colonel, awarded the DSO and bar and mentioned in despatches for his
war services. In 1937 he was created a Knight of the Thistle.
Additionally he was Lord-Lieutenant of Dumbartonshire 1919–48,
Lord Rector of Glasgow University 1934–37 and Lord High
Commissioner for the Church of Scotland in 1932 and 1940–41. He died
on 12 November 1948.

1915

Gefreiter (Lance-Corporal) Fritz Zeck, 235th Reserve Infantry Regiment was seriously wounded – and his brother killed – soon after war broke out in 1914. By the summer of 1915 he was back in the line, only to receive an extraordinary request from his company commander: with his knowledge of Dutch and his violin-playing ability, he was to find carol books and train and accompany a soldiers' choir that Christmas. He remembered:[82]

About 50 men who could 'sing' were chosen from the battalion and the practice began . . . The result was perhaps not very pleasing, but at least the carols were heard, loud and clear.

Shortly before Christmas we were ready. In the trench it was comparatively quiet with little artillery activity and isolated rifle and machine-gun fire . . . We assembled about two thirds of the rehearsed singers into the front line trench as twilight fell. We were only about 60–80 metres from the English positions.

We climbed out of the trench and sang our first carol, 'Stille Nacht, Heilige Nacht'. When the sound had faded away, we could see in the light of some flares some English on top of their breastworks listening to us. As the carols went on, more and more joined them, so that finally a large group stood listening in the open.

After we had sung all our carols we could hear a few calls from opposite which we could not quite comprehend. We too called something across and both parties disappeared into their trenches.

During this night no shot fell.

Fritz Zeck survived the war.

[82] *Christmas Truce* by Malcolm Brown and Shirley Seaton, published by Leo Cooper in 1984: reproduced by kind permission of Malcolm Brown and Shirley Seaton.

1915

John Hill Macintosh, the son of George Macintosh of Kilbarchan, Renfrewshire, enlisted in the 1st/6th (City of Glasgow) Battalion, Highland Light Infantry on 16 October 1914, leaving Queen Street Station, Glasgow for active service in the Middle East theatre on 19 February 1915. He arrived at Cape Helles, Gallipoli on 2 July 1915 and wrote in his diary five days later: 'We got the order to prepare to move. This means we are into the serious side of soldiering after many months of training.' The following day he wrote: 'Our first taste of the firing line has been not at all unpleasant. There is a fine touch of excitement in it.' His initial enthusiasm soon subsided and he wrote in his diary that Christmas:[83]

Decr 25 'A Merry Xmas' Well! Have spent worse Xmas's but not much. Have had Xmas pudding at dinner time today. It was very good altho the portion was small. Johnnie Turk has sent some shells down today. He kept at it for nearly an hour & we thought some of his HEs were going to cop us.[84] Several pieces came into our dugout. Clark is looking well today. He has a swollen ankle & has not had a shave for a good few days so is hobbling about with an old bag on his foot. He looks all the world like a Turk. Have just heard the sad news that Archie McLardie (Lieut) 5th A&SH was blown to bits with one of the HEs.

As part of the phased withdrawal of Allied troops, John Macintosh was evacuated from the Gallipoli peninsula on the night of 8/9 January 1916, writing in his diary:

We reached the rendezvous Sedall Bair [sic] about 23.30 and by 0230 on the 9th we had steam

---

[83] The papers of J. H. Macintosh in the Imperial War Museum Documents Collection: by kind permission of Helen Biele.
[84] HE – high explosive shell.

up on the HMS Prince George *and were ready to move. 'Bang'. The cruiser has been hit with something, I noticed all the sailors who were in the mess get their oilskins and go up on deck so I got up on my pins too in case there was anything doing. Heard later from the sailors that an enemy's submarine had hit us forward but the pin of the torpedo had not been released as it did not explode. A good job too for there were 1,893 troops & 750 sailors on board.*

John Macintosh's luck did not last: he was commissioned as a second lieutenant in the Highland Light Infantry and went to the trenches in France, where he was killed in action on 14 April 1917. Having no known grave, he is commemorated on the Thiépval Memorial.

1915

Getting Christmas supplies through to the troops could be a hazardous business. Having been 'Conducting Officer on the very last ferry to leave Suvla Bay', an anonymous correspondent wrote on 29 December 1915 of his harrowing experiences off Gallipoli a few nights earlier:[85]

Shortly after this I went up to V. Beach on a tramp, in charge of 10,000 Xmas Puddings.[86] *Well, we got these landed all right, though Kum Kale fired a few pip-squeaks at us, and anchored off the beach to have dinner. We had barely sat down when a Sub. Lieut. came or rather rushed in and said 'Chanak is shelling us'. Well Chanak is nasty, he fires 6 inch High Explosive.*

Barely had this chap spoken when Bang! Crash! over heeled the ship, out went the lights, biff! went the crockery and smash! went all the glass. I didn't wait for any more, but dived for my kit, which was all in a small handbag, and bunked for a lifeboat, for which everyone made. There were only 18 on board, and 1 was killed by the explosion. The remainder of us got in and rowed away from the ship. Barely had we done so than down she went — 6 inch H.E. in the engine room and blew her boilers out. She wasn't much loss anyway, being only a tiny little tramp, but think of the shock to our nerves! The Turks had no regard for that at all! I expect they think they sunk a Dreadnought. *They do so every day according to their pals the German Press.*

[85] Imperial War Museum Documents Collection: every effort has been made to trace copyright holders and the Imperial War Museum would be grateful for any information which might help to trace those whose identities or addresses are not currently known. The writer described the successful evacuation of the Suvla and Anzac sectors at Gallipoli as 'one of the greatest triumphs of Military organisation yet known'.

[86] It would be nice to think that, among these, was the one enjoyed by Private John Macintosh — see previous entry.

1915

The British Library has a collection of First World War Christmas cards, distinguished by their variety, ingenuity, humour and artistry. One card, produced on the lowest quality paper by the roneo process, was signed: 'To Mother with best wishes for Xmas and New Year 1915–16 from Rupert, I.E.F. "D", Mesopotamia.'[87] The following verses by William J. Lidwell were included:[88]

> *Greetings from an old, old Land,*
> *The warmest place on Earth:*
> *Where the fame of dear old England,*
> *Has just been given birth.*

[87] Mesopotamia, from the Greek meaning 'the land between two rivers' (the Tigris and the Euphrates), was then part of the rapidly-disintegrating Ottoman Empire. After the First World War Mesopotamia was divided up and now forms Iraq, together with parts of Syria, Turkey and Iran.

[88] First World War Christmas Cards © The British Library. All rights reserved.

Where England's sons are fighting,
Her honour to uphold;
And earning for her, glory,
By deeds both brave and bold.

From sunbaked Mesopotamia
I send these wishes true:
Good Luck and a Jolly Christmas,
With all good things for you.

And when the Old Year waneth,
May the New one to you be,
A fount of Health and Happiness,
Wealth and Prosperity.

There is a drawing of a palm tree, with an arrow pointing to the shade at its foot, and the additional message: 'May life's troubles evade you as doth the shade in Mesopotamia.'

1916

During the First World War, extensive use was made of the Field Service Post Card, which was more correctly known – in typical Army fashion – as A.F.A. 2042 114/Gen. No./5248. It was a multiple choice card that could be completed in a few moments and, furthermore, made no demands whatever on the ubiquitous censor. That Christmas Headquarters, 40th Division chose to poke fun at the process by producing a spoof Field Service Post Card:[89]

NOTHING to be written on this side except the best and brightest wishes of the sender. Sentences not required may be erased. If anything sad or sorry is added the value of the card will be destroyed.

I am quite bon.

I hope this finds you

      in the pink   *{as it leaves me.*
      fed up   *{at the present.*

I am sending this home

                A Merry Christmas
To wish you   *A Merry & Happy Christmas*
                A Happy New Year

Better follows at the first opportunity.

I hope this war will end

    this year.
    next year.
    some time.
    never.

Christian Name only

Kisses —————————————

[Any more must be sent by letter or post card if there is no more room on this card.]

Give my love to Maud, Emily, Ethel, or any other names that suits [sic] you.

[89] First World War Christmas Cards © The British Library. All rights reserved.

1917

Fed up with his work at the foundry, Thomas George Edgerton enlisted in the Army on the outbreak of war. Twenty-one year-old Gunner Edgerton was now serving in Palestine with C Battery, 301 Brigade, Royal Field Artillery, 60th (London) Division. Long after the war ended he expanded on his diary entries to write *A Christmas in the Holy Land*:[90]

Although Bethlehem was generally out of bounds I was most fortunate enough to get there . . . It was a memorable journey & according to my map I was on the ancient Pilgrim's Road. It was more of a rough track than a road & I remember wondering whether perhaps many hundreds of years before our Lord had passed this very way. The scene compared very favourably with the pictures I had seen in the Bible during my childhood. Perhaps the view had not changed very much during the last nineteen hundred years. I can remember passing through Shepherds' Field & wondered vaguely whether this was perhaps the spot where 'Shepherds watched their flocks by night' . . .

I enquired from a friendly looking Franciscan Monk the whereabouts of the dignitary I was to meet. He was very old, but most hospitable. He bowed to me most majestically & bid me welcome to the City. He was very proud of his English but I had great difficulty in understanding him. He knew where I could find the gentleman I desired to see but begged me to see inside his church before I left. He seemed very proud of it, but to me it looked shabby & neglected & gave me a feeling of sadness. It was divided into two parts by a stone pathway running down the centre, one half for the Greek Orthodox & the other for the Armenians. Each being responsible for the upkeep & cleanliness of their respective portions. Their efforts to me seemed to leave much to be desired. He even told me that the two sections did not get along well together & it was nothing for Moslem

[90] The papers of T. G. Edgerton in the Imperial War Museum Documents Collection: by kind permission of his grand-daughter, Jill Belfield.

policemen being called to break up occasional brawls. I was glad to get away from this old man who had shattered so many of my dreams, & out into the sweet fresh air. I found my dignitary & completed my mission & made my way back to the battery — and to the war.

On December 23rd we went back into action. We passed through Jerusalem again at night. We took up our position about four miles from the City on the Nablus Road. It commences to rain hard. We hear that the Turkish counter-attack is imminent. During the 24th we did our best in the appalling weather to dig ourselves in. Christmas Day dawned & the rain came down incessantly. About midday the General in charge of our division inspected our position with the C.R.A.[91] He did not like it at all & ordered us out. We were, he said, too vulnerable. We were to take up a position some eight hundred yards further back. The rain persisted with a piercing cold wind. Those six guns had to be man-handled out of the mud & on to the road before the teams could hook up & take them away. We had no mechanical aid in those days. Drenched to the skin, cold & almost exhausted our guns were eventually in position & we looked in vain for a dry spot to rest. Somebody, somehow managed to brew some tea. The C.O. ordered a rum ration. Hot tea laced with a small dose of rum & bully beef & biscuits was very welcome Christmas fare. Nobody was in festive mood. In fact I am quite sure nobody realised what the date was until afterwards. We waited throughout the night for the expected attack but it never came. The rain persisted. I am sure that was the longest, coldest and most miserable night I have ever had.

Unable to break into journalism, although his brother was publishing manager at *The Daily Mail*, Thomas Edgerton returned to the foundry, until it closed during the 1930s slump. Borrowing money from his brother, he then set up a modest lending library: with the basket on the front of his bicycle full of books, he did the rounds of the grand houses, lending to those 'below stairs'. This business dried up when the next war broke out and Thomas Edgerton became an Air Raid Protection (ARP) warden. He died on 13 February 1976.

[91] Commander Royal Artillery, the senior Royal Artillery officer in the division.

1917

Henry and Cece Giffard of Lockeridge House, near Marlborough, Wiltshire, had six sons and five daughters. All the sons served in the First World War, one in the Royal Navy and the other five in the Royal Artillery. In order of age: Henry survived the war as one of the youngest captains in the Navy; Jack was invalided out of the Army after being seriously wounded at Néry on 1 September 1914; Bob (twin), died of wounds on 1 November 1914 during the First Battle of Ypres; Eddie (twin) served on the Western Front from 1915 to 1918; Sydney was killed on 1 May 1915 at Gallipoli, while the youngest, Walter, went out to France in 1917 to join 13th Kite Balloon Section. That Christmas Eddie was out of the line, living in the *Mairie* at Habarcq, near Arras while Walter was based at 'Swan Château', near Bailleul in the Ypres sector.[92] Eddie wrote in his diary:[93]

Christmas Day! Men had a big dinner of Pork & Plum Pudding: we had our dinner in the evening: more snow: received letters from home. Seigne left for Course in England rather suddenly.

Meanwhile Walter wrote:

I can imagine them saying 'poor fellows spending Xmas in France'. Well we had a dinner party of 14 and this was the menu:

Hors d'oeuvres
Oxtail soup

[92] Possibly Château de Warande. The soldiers had a habit of anglicising place names they couldn't pronounce: for example, Plugstreet for Ploegsteert, Armenteers for Armentières, Bally-all for Bailleul and Hazy-brook for Hazebrouck.

[93] *Guns, Kites and Horses – Three Diaries from the Western Front*, edited by Sydney Giffard, published by The Radcliffe Press in 2003: reproduced by permission of the publisher.

Lobster Mayonnaise
Roast Turkey with sausages
Potatoes and Peas
Plum pudding (on fire)
Fruit jellies
Cheese straws
Coffee
'FIZZ'

I bet not many people at home had a dinner like that and in any case it is much easier for us to keep going than it is for them. We have nothing to worry us. Fritz did not bomb us for once.

Boxing Day

If there is any place more likely to make one feel Christmasie than another, I should think it is a balloon on a windy day. But Whelan and I were none the worse for being up for three hours in the afternoon. Got another parcel. Fritz started bombing again.

By 8 November 1918 it was clear to Eddie that the German Army had been defeated, as he noted in his diary:

All sorts of rumours of Armistice: Bosch deputation reported to have entered the French lines.

That was the last entry: the same day Major Edmund Hamilton Giffard was wounded in his bivouac at Les Mottes Farm by 'one of the last three shells fired by the German guns in this sector'. He died of his wounds on 10 November 1918 — less than 24 hours later the Armistice came into effect. Walter Giffard survived the war, commanded 6th Wiltshire Battalion of the Home Guard during the Second World War and died on 25 June 1970, at the age of seventy-five.

1917

In mid-August 1917, in order to prevent them becoming a rallying-point for a counter-revolution, the Kerensky government moved the Russian Imperial family from the palace of Tsarskoe Selo, near Petrograd to the former Governor's Mansion in Tobolsk, Siberia.[94] On 8 December the Tsarina wrote to Anya Vyrubova, a lady-in-waiting and her principal confidante:[95]

Here we live far from everybody and life is quiet, but we read of all the horrors that are going on. But I shall not speak of them. You live in their very centre, and that is enough for you to bear. Petty troubles surround us. The maids have been in Tobolsk four days and yet they are not allowed to come to our house, although it was promised that they should. How pitiful this everlasting suspicion and fear. I suppose it will be the same with Isa.[96] Nobody is now allowed to approach us, but I hope they will soon see how stupid and brutal and unfair it is to keep them waiting.

It is very cold — 24 degrees of frost. We shiver in the rooms, and there is always a strong draught from the windows. Your pretty jacket is so useful. We all have chilblains on our fingers. (You remember how you suffered from them in your cold little house?) I am writing this while resting before dinner. Little Jimmy lies near me while his mistress plays the piano.[97] On the 6th Alexei, Marie and Gilik acted a little play for us.[98] The others are committing to memory scenes

---

[94] Founded in 1703, St. Petersburg was known as Petrograd from 1914 to 1924, when it was renamed Leningrad; after a referendum it became St. Petersburg again in 1991.

[95] According to the Gregorian calendar, she was writing on 21 December 1917. Anya Vyrubova was imprisoned in the Peter and Paul Fortress, Petrograd, released after a number of trials, wrote *Memories of the Russian Court*, became a nun and died in Helsinki on 20 July 1964, at the age of eighty. This book is currently published by Paul Minet, Piccadilly Rare Books, 3 Apsley Court, Pickforde Lane, Ticehurst, East Sussex TN5 7BJ.

[96] Baroness Sophie Karlovna Buxhoeveden, another lady-in-waiting to the Tsarina, then lodging in Tobolsk; she was later released and fled to England.

[97] Jimmy, Anastasia's King Charles spaniel, given to her by Anya Vyrubova.

[98] Pierre Gilliard, French tutor to the five children: Olga, Tatiana, Marie and Anastasia and Alexei.

from French plays. Excellent distraction, and good for the memory. The evenings we spend together. He reads aloud to us, and I embroider. I am very busy all day preparing Christmas presents; painting ribbons for book markers, and cards as of old. I also have lessons with the children, as the priest is no longer permitted to come. But I like these lessons very much. So many things come back to my mind . . . There are some beautiful passages in the Proverbs of Solomon. The Psalms *also give me peace. Dear, we understand each other. I thank you for everything, and in memory I live over again our happy past.*

In April the members of the senior branch of the Romanov family were moved to Ekaterinburg and, on the night of 16/17 July 1918, they were all killed in the cellar of the Ipatiev House.

1917/18

Howard Couldrake was born on 8 May 1889 at Bratton, near Westbury, Wiltshire, educated at the village school and joined the Royal Marines on 16 September 1907. According to his daughter Kathleen, he 'played football and boxed for the Marines, and was champion in his weight for a few years'. By 1917 he was serving as a lance-corporal with D Company, 3rd Royal Marine Battalion at Mudros on the island of Lemnos, as part of the Salonika Expeditionary Force. He was sent as part of a detach-ment to defend the Royal Naval Air Station at Thasos and wrote in his diary: [99]

Dec 25th Tuesday. Christmas Day. As I thought we had a splendid dinner of bully beef and preserved potatoes our usual fare. I think I have tasted roast beef once since last June. We seem to be forgotten for everything on this fever stricken island, while at Headquarters at Mudros they live on the fat of the land. Football match between Marines and R.N.A.S., Marines winning 2–0.

Although the war was now over, Howard Couldrake was kicking his heels on Lemnos the following Christmas. His sense of irony had not deserted him:

Dec 25th Another very happy Xmas day, we had a splendid spread of Bully and biscuits, my thoughts are very much at home.

When he was released from the Royal Marines, Howard Couldrake returned to live at 6 Luccombe Terrace, Bratton and ran a haulage business. He died on 21 November 1968.

[99] The papers of H. T. Couldrake in the Imperial War Museum Documents Collection: by kind permission of Kathleen C. White.

1918

Before the war, Albert Robert Wilkinson worked as a piercer at Mather Lane Spinning Company at Leigh, in Lancashire. In December 1914 he enlisted in the Royal Scots Greys, transferred to the Seaforth Highlanders the following year and first came to notice for his gallant behaviour as a company runner during the Battle of the Somme. By October 1918 he was still a company runner, but was now serving with 1st/5th Manchester Regiment. The citation for his Victoria Cross reads: 'For most conspicuous bravery and devotion to duty on 20 October 1918, during the attack on Marou, when four runners in succession having been killed in an endeavour to deliver a message to the supporting company, Private Wilkinson volunteered for the duty. He succeeded in delivering the message, though the journey involved exposure to extremely heavy machine-gun and shell fire for 600 yards. He showed magnificent courage and complete indifference to danger, thinking only of the needs of his company, and entirely disregarding any consideration for personal safety. Throughout the remainder of the day Private Wilkinson continued to do splendid work.' That December Albert Wilkinson wrote to his mother:

I have got some good news for you this time. It is quite true about my decoration. I have been awarded the V.C. I feel too glad to write now, as I have just had it [the riband] *pinned on my breast by my officer. He is more proud of me than I am, nearly. I had a telegram from the Colonel yesterday to congratulate me. I will be alright now, for I shall be coming home on a month's leave as soon as I get back to the Battalion, and I will get £50 a year for life now. This is all now, so I will wish you a Merry Christmas and a Happy New Year.*

Returning from France the following February, newly-promoted Lance-Corporal Albert Wilkinson had a busy month, being invested with the Victoria Cross by HM King George V at Buckingham Palace and then attending a civic reception at Leigh. He was presented with an illuminated address and £50 by the directors of Mather Lane Spinning Company and with a gold watch by St. Joseph's Boys' and Young Men's Society. He was also given 500 War Certificates, together with £442 10s 6d, which had been raised by public subscription. After demobilisation Albert Wilkinson remained in Leigh, marrying Grace Davies in October 1932. By September 1939 he was working in the surveyor's laboratory at Bickershaw Colliery and joined the Home Guard on the outbreak of hostilities. On 18 October 1940 Albert Wilkinson was asphyxiated at the Colliery when a sparrow became wedged in a ventilation pipe.

1918

Lieutenant-Colonel Robert Joyce Clarke, a territorial officer in the Royal Berkshire Regiment, wrote from Italy to his wife on 12 January 1919:[100]

Very little has happened the last week, only two matters of interest. Firstly the rains never stopped for five days & six nights, & the rivers were all raging torrents. They were a sight, whole trees were rooted up & swept down, light bridges were washed away, & the local people were very anxious, no one had ever seen the like. I understood why the river banks are built so high & so strongly, of course the rush of water from the mountains is enormous. The current was over twelve miles an hour. The course of the river changed its side, before the flood it was on the left, after it was on the right side. I had heard before that this often happens, still it was interesting to see it. Secondly our children's party on the 6th was a great success. They all assembled in the village schoolrooms, it was to begin at 5.30 but at 4 they began to arrive! We expected about 120, when I went into the two rooms I counted over 90 in each, & a few more came in later. The Xmas tree was lighted up & we, that is the Officers & Sergeants, made a procession from the schools to the old church (this is our Canteen and concert hall etc) it holds about 350 sitting on forms etc. Each of us took a small girl, & all the rest of the kids followed on. We walked round the tree & waited, about half the Sergeants were in fancy dress, any kind of dress too! Then the Adjutant & Green, one of the Subalterns, came in dressed as Father Xmas & his wife. Here Father Xmas is not the bringer of toys etc but an old woman called 'Bifana', so our idea worked well. The Adjutant made a short speech in Italian, & then began to give away the presents from the tree. We had bought 150 presents & there were about 100 decorations on the tree too. The place was packed, for odd parents had pushed their way in too. The noise was deafening for we had a made-up band of tin

---

[100] The papers of Lieutenant-Colonel R. J. Clarke CMG DSO TD in the Imperial War Museum Documents Collection: by kind permission of Simon and Roger Warner. The citation for Robert Clarke's DSO, from the *London Gazette* of 14 November 1916, reads: 'For conspicuous gallantry in action. He has handled his battalion with great skill and determination. On three separate occasions his fine leading has achieved important success.'

trumpets, bugles, drums, any odd thing etc & they never ceased. The kids crowded round & I hope everyone got something. Then we took the tree away, & gave them cocoa, biscuits, sandwiches of bread & bully beef, cheese & jam, over 1,000 were eaten. Then we gave an entertainment of sorts, & a dancing bear, elephant, horse, dancers etc all came in & performed — the kids were a bit frightened at first, but they soon got used to them. As they went away, we gave them each two oranges & a card. They all really enjoyed themselves & I get smiles from each kid when I meet them now! The village schoolmistress is a wonderful organiser, I am sure — she has all the kids so well behaved. She sent me such a pretty little view of Venice, I think it is, in oil asking if she might be Bifana to me, a pretty idea. Tell Mother I sent her 15 photos by one of my subalterns going on leave today, they ought to arrive about the 19th. Can't think of any more news.

1931

In his poem 'Christmas in India', Rudyard Kipling summarises the sense of isolation felt by India's exiles:[101]

> *Dim dawn behind the tamarisks — the sky is saffron-yellow —*
> *As the women in the village grind the corn,*
> *And the parrots seek the river-side, each calling to his fellow*
> *That the Day, the staring Eastern Day is born.*
> *O the white dust on the highway! O the stenches in the byway!*
> *O the clammy fog that hovers over earth!*
> *And at Home they're making merry 'neath the white and scarlet berry —*
> *What part have India's exiles in their mirth?*
>
> *Full day behind the tamarisks — the sky is blue and staring —*
> *As the cattle crawl afield beneath the yoke,*
> *And they bear One o'er the field-path, who is past all hope or caring,*
> *To the ghât below the curling wreaths of smoke.*
> *Call on Rama, going slowly, as ye bear a brother lowly —*
> *Call on Rama — he may hear, perhaps, your voice!*
> *With our hymn-books and our psalters we appeal to other altars,*
> *And to-day we bid 'good Christian men rejoice!'*

[101] From *East of Suez*, published by Macmillan in 1931. Kipling knew what it was like to be an exile: named after Rudyard Lake in Staffordshire, he was born in Bombay in 1865, left India to be educated in England at the age of six, rejoined his parents in Lahore eleven years later, left India for good in 1889, married and went to live in Vermont in 1892, finally returning to England four years later, after a quarrel with his brother-in-law.

High noon behind the tamarisks — the sun is hot above us —
As at Home the Christmas Day is breaking wan.
They will drink our healths at dinner — those who tell us how they love us,
And forget us till another year be gone!
O the toil that knows no breaking! O the Heimweh, ceaseless, aching!
O the black dividing Sea and alien Plain!
Youth was cheap — wherefore we sold it. Gold was good — we hoped to hold it,
And to-day we know the fulness of our gain.

Grey dusk behind the tamarisks — the parrots fly together —
As the Sun is sinking slowly over Home;
And his last ray seems to mock us shackled in a lifelong tether
That drags us back howe'er so far we roam.
Hard her service, poor her payment — she in ancient, tattered raiment —
India, she the grim Stepmother of our kind.
If a year of life be lent her, if her temple's shrine we enter,
The door is shut — we may not look behind.

Black night behind the tamarisks — the owls begin their chorus —
As the conches from the temple scream and bray.
With the fruitless years behind us, and the hopeless years before us,
Let us honour, O my brothers, Christmas Day!
Call a truce, then, to our labours — let us feast with friends and neighbours,
And be merry as the custom of our caste;
For if 'faint and forced the laughter,' and if sadness follow after,
We are richer by one mocking Christmas past.

1934

Newly-commissioned John Masters describes his experiences when first attached to the 1st Battalion, Duke of Cornwall's Light Infantry at Bareilly in northern India:[102]

I can live with the memory of my first day in the awe-inspiring and gloomy splendour of an officers' mess. It was in Bareilly, and I was still nineteen. I sat down to tea at the polished table and cautiously admired a large fruit cake in front of me. After licking my lips for five minutes, I screwed up my courage and asked the captain next to me whether I might be allowed to have some cake. He turned, looked at me with an indescribable expression of scorn and astonishment, and said coldly, 'Yes. That's a mess cake. You're not at your prep school now.'

Christmas came. I had ceased to be nineteen, and on Christmas Day it was my turn to be orderly officer. On this day my duties included following the colonel, the second-in-command, and the adjutant round every mess hall in the battalion — seven of them — and, in each mess, drinking toasts from half-tumblers of whisky thinly diluted with fizzy lemonade. The British soldiers, far from home and families, tried to forget their exile in a riot of snowballing, singing and drinking. The sergeants waited on them at table.

After a couple of hours our bedraggled and hardly conscious convoy reached the officers' mess and sat down, without hunger, before an enormous Christmas dinner. The lieutenant at the head of the table suddenly remembered that this day was traditionally a topsy-turvy one for rank and discipline. He picked a leg of turkey off his plate and flung it accurately at the officer sitting at the other end, who happened to be a senior major. The colonel smiled, but after all he was no longer in his twenties. He collected the majors with his eye and left us. As the field officers crept silently out the air grew thick with flying potatoes, pudding, turkey, gravy, and oranges.

I watched in amazement. If we had behaved like this at the Royal Military College we would have been rusticated on the spot and told we were quite unfit to be officers. Apparently when one

[102] *Bugles and a Tiger*, published by Michael Joseph in 1956: reproduced by permission of Pollinger Limited and the proprietor.

actually became an officer the rules were different. Amazement gave place to loneliness and a despair born of all those toasts, for I was not at all used to drinking. I have tried so hard to be an officer, I thought tearfully. I wanted so much to be treated as one of the family. But no-one is throwing anything at me. *They haven't forgiven me about the cake yet. Then — oh, ecstasy! — hard fingers were rubbing brandy butter into my hair and stuffing Christmas pudding into my ears. I was forgiven, accepted! I flung myself with abandon into the riot, and the steaming rum punch flew faster round the table and the snow flew thicker outside the windows.*

During the Second World War John Masters was awarded the DSO for his period in command of 111th Indian Infantry Brigade during a fiercely-fought Chindit operation in northern Burma.[103] After the war he left the Army, emigrated to the United States and became a full-time author, writing mainly about India and the British Raj. John Masters died in 1983.

---

[103] The Chindits were a long-range penetration force, founded by Major-General Orde Wingate, and named after the *Chinthe*, the mythical winged stone lions that guard the entrances to Buddhist temples.

1939

The now-traditional Christmas broadcast was inaugurated by HM King George V in 1932 but the first to make a real impact was the one given by his second son shortly after the outbreak of war. Dressed in the uniform of an Admiral of the Fleet, HM King George VI sat in front of two microphones at Sandringham and said: 'A new year is at hand. We cannot tell what it will bring. If it brings peace, how thankful we shall be. If it brings continued struggle we shall remain undaunted. In the meantime I feel that we may all find a message of encouragement in the lines, which, in my closing words, I should like to say to you:

> I said to the man
> who stood at the gate of the year,
> 'Give me a light that I may tread safely
> into the unknown.'
>
> And he replied,
> 'Go out into the darkness
> and put your hand into the hand of God.
> That shall be to you
> better than light
> and safer than a known way!'
>
> So I went forth
> and finding the hand of God,
> trod gladly into the night.

The BBC was besieged with enquiries about the poem but the King did not know the author: he had quoted from the last part of a longer poem, sent to him on a Christmas card. The author – who had heard the broadcast but not immediately recognised her own words – was Minnie Louise Haskins, a Sunday school teacher and later lecturer in Social Sciences at the London School of Economics, who had written the poem in 1908.

One result of the broadcast was the first publication of a collection of Louise Haskins's poetry.[104] Another was that, capitalising on public enthusiasm, J. Arthur Rank produced a film at Denham Studios. It was a re-working of an earlier Rank picture called *Turn of the Tide* and ends with the family listening to a broadcast, in which a recording of the King's speech was used.

[104] Extract from *The Gate of the Year* by Minnie Louise Haskins (copyright © M. Louise Haskins, 1908) is reproduced by permission of Sheil Land Associates Ltd on behalf of the Estate of M. Louise Haskins.

1939

Both before, and during, the London Blitz Vera Reid, then in her late 40s, worked with the Women's Voluntary Service. Among other things she helped with the evacuation of pregnant women and schoolchildren, the distribution of gas masks and the resettlement of French and Belgian refugees. That first Christmas at war she wrote in her diary:[105]

Christmas trees for those who shelter in the tubes. And a special train to bring Christmas dinner. How quickly it has all become an organised part of life this living in shelters. At first confusion was bad. People rushed out when the all clear sounded and then went back again at once so that they spent all day and all night below ground. Then came the time when no one was allowed to stake a claim for the night before 4 o'clock. I used to watch them on my way to the club waiting on the platform with large bundles of luggage until the time came when they could get settled down. After that tickets were issued and bunks put up. The bunks were a great improvement. Before that people used to sleep two deep against the walls of the stations while others lay in rows with their feet pointing towards the rails. In consequence there was only just room to walk along the edge of the platform. Not a nice feeling when the train was moving.

The night life differs in every tube station. At St. James's Park all is very decorous and quiet. Everyone is asleep or at least lying down when I pass there at night. At Piccadilly there is much more life and variety. People play games, have parties and meet together. At Leicester Square they eat sausages and play toss half penny. Baker Street is lively but dull. No cards or games and sleeping people.

At Piccadilly there is a young couple who come every night. I have watched their baby grow. He can sit up now. When he first came he was always asleep. A girl who sits opposite them writes

[105] The papers of Miss V. Reid in the Imperial War Museum Documents Collection: every effort has been made to trace copyright holders and the author and the Imperial War Museum would be grateful for any information which might help to trace those whose identities or addresses are not currently known.

pages and pages every night. I wonder if she's a journalist or if it's love letters she writes. I think it's letters. But what can she find to say. For whether I go home early or late there she is always writing away as if her life depended upon it. Then there is the old man with tin spectacles and a red handkerchief. He wears mittens and when I first noticed him, was learning to knit. Putting the wool laboriously over each stitch and holding thick needles. Now he knits gloves . . .

1940

After Dunkirk the Children's Overseas Reception Board (CORB) was set up to organise the evacuation of children from Britain for the duration of the war. There were other schemes – and private arrangements as well – but all were brought to an end when the SS *City of Benares*, flagship of the Ellerman Line, was torpedoed and sunk by U-48 on 17 September 1940. Of the ninety CORB children on board, only thirteen survived. Alistair Horne was one of around 5,000 children to go to America, where he lived with John and Rossy Cutler and their children at 58 East 80th Street, New York and also at Post Road Farm, Garrison-on-Hudson.[106] Of the end of an interrupted school year – spent partly at Stowe in Buckinghamshire, and then at Millbrook School, upstate New York – he wrote:[107]

Swiftly on the heels of Thanksgiving came the end of term. It was dignified, as of tradition, by Mr Pulling reading the whole of A Christmas Carol *to the entire school.[108] 'To the graduated dismay of all who had heard the story one, or twice, or three times', commented Bill Buckley in the years to come. But Mr Pulling read it with such personal enjoyment, so mellifluously with that agreeably mid-Atlantic accent, that it never failed to make me feel nearer to home. In 1940, Dickens was succeeded, in the last chapel of term, by the Boss choosing as the text of his sermon King George VI's famous Christmas broadcast of 1939: 'And I said to the Man who stood at the Gate of the Year . . .'*

[106] Sir Alistair Horne is a biographer of Harold Macmillan and Francophile commentator on many of the major recent events in French history – Paris and the Commune 1870–71, Verdun 1916, the Fall of France 1940 and Algeria 1954–62 – with the objectivity and perceptiveness only truly permitted to a outsider.

[107] *A Bundle from Britain*, published by Macmillan in 1993: by kind permission of Sir Alistair Horne CBE.

[108] Headmaster of Millbrook School, where Alistair Horne studied for three years.

1940

Pilot Officer Hugh 'Cocky' Dundas had flown his *Spitfire* over the beaches of Dunkirk and claimed his first combat victory on 7 July. He was shot down over Kent on 22 August and heard the news of his brother's disappearance over the Channel on 28 November. He was spending Christmas in Yorkshire, where his family lived:[109]

Christmas Day. Last night I went to Wortley for dinner. It was the same as it always has been.[110] *I got there five minutes late, but five minutes before anybody came downstairs. Moss produces the sherry; it is always the same formula 'Good evening, Master Hughie; I think they're all upstairs changing yet, sir. I'll get the sherry, sir. Have you got everything you want, Master Hughie?' And then Archie stumps down, and Elfin, and Barbara and Diana, always late.*[111] *And Diana looks even more beautiful than usual; and one half of me says you're in love, you fool, tell her, while the other half says you've no right to be in love with anybody. And tonight I almost did tell her and then stopped and felt a fool. But of course she knows and then I think she could be persuaded to love me. But then I am back full circle at the unanswerable argument that in my present occupation I can't make girls like Diana love me.*

We went to church at 8 o'clock. No church bells, no rows of candles on the High Altar; just an improvised table with two shaded candles, and a hidden congregation in the dark church: Holy Communion on Christ's birthday hiding secretly from German bombs. It is one thousand nine hundred years exactly since the first Supper Feast, and we have to celebrate like this, like Roman Christians in the Catacombs.

[109] *Flying Start, A Fighter Pilot's War Years*, published by Stanley Paul in 1988: reproduced by kind permission of The Random House Group Ltd.

[110] It wasn't to remain the same for that much longer: on 5 May 1951 Wortley Hall, formerly home to the Earl and Countess of Wharncliffe, was formally opened as an educational and holiday centre for the Trades Union, Labour and Co-operative Movements. In the words of the current President: 'This is our oasis of socialism, let us ensure its successful continuation.'

[111] The Wharncliffes and two of their daughters; Diana married the 9th Duke of Newcastle in 1946.

During the war Hugh Dundas was awarded the DSO and bar, as well as the DFC. His post-war career was no less distinguished: he was knighted and served as Chairman of Thames Television 1981–87. Sir Hugh Dundas died on 10 July 1995.

1940

Having resigned as First Lord of the Admiralty on 3 October 1938 in protest at the Munich agreement, Duff Cooper was appointed Minister of Information in Winston Churchill's coalition government in May 1940. On 22 December his wife, Lady Diana, wrote to their son John Julius from Ditchley Park in Oxfordshire, the country house belonging to Ronald Tree, who had previously been Duff Cooper's Parliamentary Private Secretary:[112]

We've got here, thank God! You should have seen the party leaving the Dorchester — Wadey staggering under sordid paper-parcels, last-minute sponges, slippers poking out, two tin hats, two gas-masks, guns, ammunition, a white Christmas tree in a red box, another Ministry red box, big boxes, little boxes, fur gloves, a terribly intimate hot-water-bottle of an poisonous green, and Papa himself twice the size of M. Michelin, in two coats under his fur coat, a muffler round his throat, another over his head and ears, a hat on top of that and only one bright little blue eye goggling out. [113]

I wish he could have a real holiday. He has not had a week except for flu since France fell. He's tired, poor boy. Winston never is, but he does all his work from bed and sleeps after lunch in pyjamas, works again from his bed, gets up for dinner and feels like a daisy at 2 a.m. when others are exhausted. Clemmie seems blissful. She can't understand those who write from the United States in pitying vein. 'Why are they sorry for us?' I quite see why they are. Clemmie, wife of the greatest of living men who finds himself beyond his life's ambition and knows that he can save us and triumph, exults in his unswerving confidence and is less to be pitied than some poor gnomes whose husbands have thankless jobs that they hate, or whose sons are fated.

Replaced at the Ministry of Information by Brendan Bracken in July

---

[112] *Trumpets from the Steep*, published by Rupert Hart-Davis in 1960: reprinted by kind permission of Ms Artemis Cooper.
[113] Wadey — Kate Wade, who had been Lady Diana Cooper's personal maid since 1915.

1941, Duff Cooper retained a place in the Cabinet as Chancellor of the Duchy of Lancaster, was briefly resident minister with responsibility for Far Eastern affairs, based in Singapore, and later British representative to the French Committee of National Liberation in Algiers, before becoming Ambassador in Paris in September 1944. He remained in post in Paris until the end of 1947, when he retired and devoted himself to his writing. Duff Cooper, who was created Viscount Norwich on 5 July 1952, died on 1 January 1954 on board the French liner *Colombie*, while on a cruise to Jamaica.

1940

Theodora Fitzgibbon, author of over thirty books, most of them on the subject of cookery – including *The Food of the Western World* – lived in London during the Blitz:[114]

The raids were very bad in Chelsea before and after Christmas: the weather was beastly cold, food scarce, and what festivity there was took place in the pubs. But this after-Christmas night I wanted to stay home, read by the fire, and finish the remains of the meagre Christmas food and drink. The anti-aircraft guns rattled the windows and the clear, frosty air intensified the whine of the bombs, which were very close. The German bombers liked clear, frosty nights. Although not heavy smokers, when a raid was bad we chain-smoked, and by ten o'clock were down to our last. The pub next door was shut, for it was closing time, and the old couple who ran it never gave a moment overtime, so there was nothing for it but to walk up to the slot machine in the King's Road . . . We hurried on to find a cordon around the Six Bells, and massive chunks of heavy masonry on the ground. The front part upstairs had been hit, and toppled into both the road and the garden a matter of minutes before closing time. People were trapped in the back . . .

Several dazed but unhurt people were led out by torchlight; one had a bottle of brandy which was passed round, and we all had a swig. Some were 'regulars' who recognised us. The one with the purloined bottle said jauntily: 'What happened to you tonight that you didn't cop this lot?' There were more inside, trapped, probably dead, as they had been sitting near the front door. Curly, the Irish barman, had gone down to the cellar and was found, his rimless spectacles still on his snub nose, but he was stone dead, an unbroken bottle in his hand. Almost-full pints of beer were standing unspilt on tables in front of customers who stared at them with unseeing eyes, for they too were dead from the blast. Similar occurrences happened every day all over London, and one learned never to persuade anyone against their will to go to a certain place.

It was towards the end of this same Christmas week that the great fire and bombing raid on the

[114] Extract from *With Love*, published by Century in 1982: reproduced by permission of David Higham Associates Ltd.

City of London took place, when the Guildhall, eight beautiful Wren churches, Guy's Hospital and hundreds of office buildings were hit, but as it was on Sunday, the latter were mercifully empty. Fire watchers saw twenty-eight incendiary bombs fall on the roof of St Paul's Cathedral, and bounce off the dome. One was blazing, and miraculously fell outwards, where it was extinguished. Indeed, amidst the wall of flame and smoke the only clear sky was around the cathedral. Londoners with a new-found love of their city watched its survival from rooftops both near and far away. With tears running down their cheeks, they said in one voice: 'The old church stood it . . .'

Theodora Fitzgibbon was awarded the Prix Choucroute First Prize for European Food Journalists at Bonn in 1987 and died in 1991.

1940

Myles Hildyard was serving with The Nottinghamshire Yeomanry (Sherwood Rangers) in Palestine. In a letter to his parents at Flintham Hall, Nottinghamshire, he wrote:[115]

Did you listen to the carols from Bethlehem on Christmas Eve? If so, you heard me. I think it is broadcast every year, generally they sing in a little courtyard surrounded by high walls against the church. We arranged for a lot of the men to go up, but the District Commissioner forbade anyone to attend the evening services at Bethlehem and we had to cancel. However Micky Riviere and I went up to Jerusalem in the evening and on to Bethlehem with Flash Kellett and two others.[116] We found the carols were being sung in a tiny chapel of St. George in a corner of the courtyard, but we were turned out as not having been invited. So we waited in the courtyard under the tower of the old Greek monastery and the planet Jupiter shining as brightly as ever the star of the Magi could have done, straight up above. Eventually the High Commissioner arrived with a large party and the American consul with another. I followed in and sat down behind Araminta.[117] None of the others managed to get in. It was a bare chapel with three or four rows of chairs for the guests and round the microphone at one end a nondescript collection of waif-like persons waiting to sing. They sang quite well and we sang too. It was very enjoyable.

I slept at the King David Hotel, which is extremely grand and incredibly expensive. I only got a room by saying I could perfectly well sleep in Dan Ranfurly's room for nothing – he being away – though Jerusalem and the King David seemed unusually empty.[118] It was nice to wake up on Christmas Day with the sun shining outside on a dome, instead of in this camp, which in fact

[115] Extract from *It Is Bliss Here* (© the Estate of Myles Hildyard, 2005) is reproduced by kind permission of Peters Fraser & Dunlop Group Ltd, on behalf of the Estate of Myles Hildyard.
[116] His Commanding Officer, Lieutenant-Colonel Edward Orlando 'Flash' Kellett DSO MP, who was killed in action in Tunisia on 22 March 1943. The Conservative member of Parliament for Birmingham Aston, he was one of twenty-three MPs killed in action during the Second World War.
[117] Araminta MacMichael, daughter of the High Commissioner.
[118] See the entry for Hermione Ranfurly in 1942.

was the point of the expedition. At ten o'clock after a sunny breakfast looking out on the walls,
Micky and I went to the Protestant Cathedral of St. George, a Victorian church, ordinary parish
size and ugly. It was a very good service, and the Anglican bishop in Jerusalem preached. I'm told
he has only been in the Church ten years and is a very great scholar. He is like a mediaeval monk.
He reads his sermons from notes — quite excellent. At the same time he employs gesticulation to
a degree which the utmost impetuosity could not save from melodrama. Thus throwing himself back
with his hands upraised from his frilly sleeves, he will come to the end of a page of his notes.
Keeping one arm absolutely steady he pauses in the middle of a great declaration, quickly turns
over his notes, and continues with undiminished vigour. He would be great in a big church where
one cannot see all this, but even as it was I was very impressed. His text was 'and there was no
room at the inn'.

Myles Hildyard was one of the few British and Commonwealth soldiers
to escape from the debacle on Crete in May 1941, eventually reaching
Turkey by boat in early September — he was awarded the Military
Cross. Having returned to Egypt, he later wrote: 'Monty came and
gave everyone medals; he couldn't be a sweeter thing, rather like Aunt
Muriel.' Myles Hildyard died on 13 August 2005.

1940

Evelyn Waugh was born in 1903, younger son of Arthur Waugh, managing director of publishers Chapman & Hall, and was educated at Lancing and Hertford College, Oxford. After just two terms teaching at a preparatory school in Wales, he decided to earn a living with his pen. In 1939 he joined the Royal Marines. He wrote to his wife Laura on Christmas Day from the SS *Glenroy*, in which No. 8 Commando was sailing to Egypt via South Africa:[119]

I am very sorry not to have written more often. We were living in very overcrowded circumstances when it was almost impossible to find space to write, but the main reason is that, under censorship, there is very little I can write without embarrassment. Now they have moved us for Christmas into a large and, for officers & sergeants, comfortable ship. Our lives are still frustrated at every turn but I have come to believe that all service life is like this, the only difference being whether one is in amusing company or not. Robin now lives a life among staff officers & we see very little of him. Harry maintains unfailing humour – a most delicious character. We never see Bob. David Stirling has joined us – a gentleman obsessed by the pleasures of chance.[120] He effectively wrecked Ludo as a game of skill & honour. Now we race clockwork motor cars. At present I am well up on the betting.

His military experiences formed the basis for some of his finest work, leading to such unforgettable characters as Guy Crouchback, Apthorpe and Trimmer in the *Sword of Honour* trilogy. Described by Graham Greene as 'the greatest novelist of his generation', Evelyn Waugh died on Easter Day 1966, after attending Mass with his family.

[119] 'Royal Marines, from the SS Glenroy' from *The Letters of Evelyn Waugh*, reprinted by permission of Sterling Lord Literistic Inc. Copyright © 1982 the Estate of Evelyn Waugh.
[120] Founder of the Special Air Service, whose parachute wings are modelled on the stylised wings of Isis, the Egyptian goddess of rebirth, on the walls of Shepheard's Hotel in Cairo (destroyed by fire in 1952).

1940

Gwenda Morgan, who was born at Petworth, Sussex on 1 February 1908, and educated at Goldsmiths' College of Art, soon established a reputation for herself as a painter and wood-engraver. During the war she lived with her father, her stepmother Una, and a number of evacuees at Old Bank House, Petworth. On 1 June 1939 the Women's Land Army was formed and Gwenda Morgan was in one of the first two groups of 'Land Girls' trained prior to the outbreak of war. She started work at Hallgate just a week before Britain declared war on Germany, on a salary of just 28 shillings a week.[121] In her diary Gwenda Morgan wrote:[122]

Dec. 24 Poultry. Dung spreading. Miserable day, dull. Asked about Christmas holiday, Mr W. said Boxing Day wasn't considered to be holiday for men but I could have it if I liked, so I said I would like and thanked him very much.[123] I didn't really think the men would have to work on Boxing Day, but at 5 o'c I saw pigman and he said, yes, and that Mr W. hadn't told them they must until the middle of the afternoon. No Christmas feeling on the farm at all. Wretched. I felt quite miserable in spite of the prospect of two days' holiday. Felt alright when I got home, though. Went up to Helen and May Austin with present (chocs) and then decorated house with holly. Hope the war will be over this time next year. O! how I hope. Package of my pictures arrived from Green & Stone (one cut by flying glass in a raid).[124] If only I had the chance of painting now, I could do something much better than these, I am sure.

By July 1943 the Women's Land Army numbered 87,000, with over 4,000 joining every month. On 8 May 1945 Gwenda Morgan wrote in her diary:

---

[121] For many Land Girls, half of this amount was deducted for board and lodging.

[122] *Diary of a Land Girl 1939–45*, published by The Whittington Press in 2002: reprinted by kind permission of John Randle, The Whittington Press.

[123] Mr Webber of Frog Farm, to which Gwenda Morgan moved from Hallgate on 21 May 1940.

[124] *Green & Stone*: picture framers and suppliers of specialist art materials, at 259 Kings Road, Chelsea since 1934.

VE DAY Yes, Victory in Europe. Good. Went to farm just to do poultry. Rest of day holiday. Put up flags, walked round town with Una, and up to Baxter's (their boy has just arrived home from prison camps in Poland and Germany). Una gave them apples and Christmas pudding — the one thing he was looking forward to as a treat. Very lively time in Market Sq. Mr Card's radio van just under our drawing-room window. Dancing in the Square till 12.15 midnight. Amusing to watch! but wouldn't liked to have been in it with soldiers rather drunk and jitter-bugging, and letting off thunder-flashes in the middle of the people. Mrs Brash got her leg burnt and veins broken, and some of the children were very frightened. Heard the King's speech, also Mr Churchill's.

Gwenda Morgan left Frog Farm in May 1946 and later wrote: 'After nearly seven years of farmwork I was glad to get back to wood-engraving.' The Women's Land Army was finally disbanded on 21 October 1950, following a parade at Buckingham Palace of over 500 Land Girls in front of HM Queen Elizabeth, who said:

I have always admired their courage in responding so readily to a call which they knew must bring them hardship and sometimes loneliness. Now the time has come to say goodbye, because the job has been done, but the sadness which many feel should be outweighed by pride in the achievement.

Gwenda Morgan never married and died at Petworth on 9 January 1991.

1941

The port of Tobruk in Libya played a key role in the titanic struggle in the Western Desert between the British and Commonwealth Eighth Army and Rommel's Deutsches Afrikakorps. The beleaguered garrison endured a siege lasting 240 days, before being relieved on 10 December 1941.[125] While serving with 153 (London) Heavy Anti-Aircraft Battery, which had played a full part in the successful defence, Gunner Dick Haydon composed a poem:[126]

Xmas Day in the Desert – Tobruk 1941

'Twas Xmas day in the desert,
The place was bleak and drear,
And all the Gunners' faces
Were not aglow with beer.

For 12 months in the desert
Amidst the toil and strife,
Without their beer and comforts
Had soured each sweet life.

---

[125] On 21 June 1942, in what Winston Churchill described as 'a hideous and unexpected shock', Tobruk surrendered. On 2 July 1942, following a two-day debate, the Prime Minister comfortably survived the motion of 'No Confidence', which had been proposed by fellow Conservative MP, Sir John Wardlaw-Milne. By contrast, Hitler promoted Erwin Rommel to Generalfeldmarschall on 22 June 1942.

[126] The papers of R. G. Haydon in the Imperial War Museum Documents Collection: every effort has been made to trace copyright holders and the author and the Imperial War Museum would be grateful for any information which might help to trace those whose identities or addresses are not currently known. This poem is loosely based on *Christmas Day in the Cookhouse* by the inter-war music hall comedian Billy Bennett. The original version is one of the songs in Joan Littlewood's satirical musical entertainment of 1963, *Oh! What a Lovely War*.

And now, at last, 'twas Xmas
That day of Xmas pud,
When each man should be sozzled,
And more so if he could.

Alas for that great dinner,
Instead of grub so nice,
The Gunners only saw a pile
Of bully beef and rice.

And then in 'crowning' glory
The Major did appear,
To tell the boys of their good work
And curse the lack of beer.[127]

You've all done damn good work, Boys
And giv'n the Hun a bashin',
So for your Xmas dinner
You'll get a double ration.

This set the men a'talking
And frowning quite a lot,
They'd all worked hard — and this reward
Just hit them like a shot.

Until with one accord they said
In words that were a farce:
'Just keep your Xmas dinner, Sir,
And stick it up your vase??!!'[128]

---

[127] The Battery Commander was Major C. F. Barrett.
[128] Dick Haydon noted that 'a slight deviation has been used from the original writing'!

1941

Squadron-Leader Donald Hill was based at Kai Tak when the Japanese attacked Hong Kong on 8 December 1941, destroying four of the five British aircraft that day. Donald Hill kept a diary – written in code – which was not translated until 1996, eleven years after his death:[129]

What a Xmas day, empty stomachs, tired out and heaven knows what is going on. At 10 a.m. a message arrives saying there is a truce until midday. This news is immediately followed by a terrific bombardment of our positions. Not my idea of a truce. More Canadians melt away leaving our line practically undefended. I gather the few remaining men together and proceed to climb Mount Gough hoping to join up with our main forces. When we reach the top and strike the main road we run into several hundred Canadians retreating from Wanchai Gap. Wanchai Gap is the most vital sector of all and this means the end. We are told that the island surrendered at 3.30 p.m., over an hour ago. The troops have no arms and are completely worn out. A scene I will never forget with ammunition dumps going up everywhere and the Japs pouring hundreds of shells just over our heads into blocks of houses across the road. Finally the barrage stops and white flags appear from all the houses. The troops have got hold of quantities of beer and are singing to relieve their shattered nerves. I am too stunned to describe my own feelings but decide to try and escape. The Japs are reputed never to take prisoners. With Junior and three of my men we grab an Austin Seven and decide to make a dash for Aberdeen to try to get a boat. The engine won't start but it's all downhill. By now it is dark and the road is very narrow and tricky. We throw away our arms and get aboard. What a ride, crashing through barbed wire and road blocks in the dark but the old Austin showed her worth and we finally coasted into Aberdeen without seeing any Japs. We go straight to the AIS and get hold of a Chinese boy who says he will try to get us a boat with food and water. Then, to our horror, we discovered that the building had been locked and we could not get out as the Japs were outside. What a disappointment and we had nothing to do except find

---

[129] Reproduced by kind permission of the translator, Dr Philip Aston of the Department of Mathematics and Statistics, University of Surrey, Guildford.

somewhere to sleep, not having had a real one for ten days. My old room was a complete shambles so slept on the floor.

On 6 February 1942 he wrote:

Spend hours these days thinking of home and family, especially Pam. They probably think I am dead and I pray to God that the Japs will get news through. Thank God for you Pammy darling, your memory is ever with me. I still have your photograph, signet ring and cigarette case. I will never lose them.

The key to the numerical code lay in the thirty-four letters in two names, those of Donald Samuel Hill and his fiancée, Pamela Seely Kirrage: they were married in 1946.

1941

The authorities had a rather different view of the Hong Kong situation from that of Squadron-Leader Donald Hill. Sir Mark Young, the Governor of Hong Kong, said:

In pride and admiration I send my greetings this Christmas Day to all who are fighting and to all who are working so nobly and so well to sustain Hong Kong against the assault of the enemy. Fight on. Hold on, for King and Empire. God bless you all in this your finest hour.

From Fortress HQ under Victoria Barracks, Major-General C. M. Maltby, the General Officer Commanding, sent the following message to the garrison:

Christmas greetings to you all. Let this day be historical in the great annals of our Empire. The Order of the Day is 'Hold Fast'.

The headline in the *South China Morning Post* was:

Day of Good Cheer

Hong Kong is observing the strangest and most sober Christmas in its centuries-old history . . . All are cheerful in the knowledge that, for all the hardships, they would not go either hungry or thirsty this Christmas.

From the other side of Hong Kong Harbour, the Japanese continued to broadcast by loudspeaker:

A merry Christmas to the gallant British soldiers. You have fought a good fight, but you are outnumbered. Now is the time to surrender. If you don't, within 24 hours we will give you all that we've got.[130]

'Marco Polo', a local newspaper reporter, wrote of the morning service at St. John's Cathedral:

The two English clergymen were bravely performing their offices despite the bombing and the shelling. The explosions came from just behind the Cathedral. I was glad when the service was over.[131]

At 7 p.m. on Christmas Day Major-General Maltby ordered British and Commonwealth Forces to surrender.

---

[130] *The Battle for Hong Kong 1941–1945* by Oliver Lindsay, published by Spellmount in 2005.
[131] *The Hidden Years* by John Luff, published by the South China Morning Post in 1967.

1941

When war broke out, Drummond Hunter was studying History and Law at Edinburgh University. A member of the University Officer Training Corps, he joined the Army and was posted to the 2nd Battalion, The Royal Scots in Hong Kong. In the summer of 1941 he met and became engaged to Peggie Scotcher, who had once studied ballet under Margot Fonteyn, but was now a volunteer nurse at the British Military Hospital. When the Japanese invaded Hong Kong, Lieutenant Drummond Hunter, his Battalion's Intelligence Officer, soon found himself in the thick of the action: he was wounded in the shoulder and arm and evacuated to Hong Kong Island. On Christmas Eve the ambulance moving him between hospitals crashed during an air raid and Drummond Hunter was thrown out of the vehicle, breaking his back in the process. At 8 p.m. on Christmas Day, just one hour after Major-General C. M. Maltby had signed the instrument of surrender, Drummond Hunter and Peggie Scotcher were married in the British Military Hospital. There were just five witnesses to the ceremony, which took place during an air raid. He later said:[132]

It was truly bizarre. The bride and Chaplain ducking under my bed as the bombs fell. Me immobile with a mattress over me for protection. We had the nurses' Christmas cake and a glass of champagne from the remaining unsmashed bottle.

Drummond Hunter remained in hospital for almost a year while Peggie was immediately sent to Stanley Civilian Internment Camp. Later he was moved to the Argyle Street Camp and later to

[132] Reproduced by kind permission of Ann Donald, whose interview was published in *The Sunday Herald*, 24 February 2002.

Shamshuipo, both on the Kowloon Peninsula. Each month he was allowed to send her a note of just twenty-five words. They were released in August 1945 and, on return to Scotland, enjoyed a belated honeymoon on Loch Earn. Of his wartime captivity Drummond Hunter said: 'Unlike the mainland prison camps, the Japanese in Hong Kong mostly tried to obey the Geneva Convention . . . You have to forgive, because hatred corrodes you.' Drummond Hunter later enjoyed a distinguished career in public service, for which he was awarded the OBE, and died on 13 April 2002.

1941

Count Galeazzo Ciano was married to Benito Mussolini's elder daughter, Edda. On 10 June 1936, at the improbably young age of 33, he became Italian Minister of Foreign Affairs, serving in that position until 8 February 1943. On Christmas Day he wrote in his diary:[133]

Alfieri writes that the disasters on the Russian front have gone farther than is desirable for us.[134] *I glean this from the Germans at the embassy. They are very much discouraged. The Duce, who in the beginning underestimated the problem, now says that it is serious and that perhaps it will have further consequences.*

The Pope has delivered a Christmas address and naturally it did not please Mussolini because he found that out of the five points it contains at least four that are directed against the dictatorships. This is unavoidable, in view of the anti-Catholic policy of the Germans. Isabella Colonna told me last evening that she had recently spoken with Cardinal Maglione, who told her that at the Vatican the Russians are preferred over the Nazis.[135]

Anyway, the Duce increasingly reveals his anti-Christian attitude. The Christmas holidays provide him with a pretext. 'For me,' he said, 'Christmas is nothing more than the 25th of December. I am the man who in the entire world feels these religious anniversaries the least.' To prove it he has made a list of appointments that is longer than usual. This year, however, the crowds in the churches are overflowing.

On 9 February 1943 Ciano became Italian Ambassador to the Holy See. At a meeting of the Fascist Grand Council on 25 July 1943, he voted against his father-in-law. Less than two months later, following the invasion of Italy by the Allies, Galeazzo Ciano was arrested by the Germans, having been persuaded that they would help him to reach

[133] *Ciano's Diary 1937–43*, published by Phoenix Press in 2002.
[134] Dino Alfieri, Italian Ambassador to Germany.
[135] Isabella Colonna, wife of Prince Piero Colonna, Governor of Rome.

Spain – and safety. Having been held for three months in Verona Jail, he and four others were charged with high treason and, after a public trial, they were executed by firing squad on 11 January 1944.[136] Edda Ciano never remarried and died in Rome on 8 April 1995.

---

[136] Count Galeazzo Ciano's son, Fabrizio, later wrote a book called *Quando il nonno fece fucilare papà* or *When Grandpa had Daddy shot*.

1941

Having begun his service with the Royal Ulster Rifles, Brian Spiller was briefly attached to B Company, 8th Battalion, Durham Light Infantry in the aftermath of Dunkirk, before sailing out to India. Attached to 1st Gurkhas, he went to Iraq as an Intelligence Officer, spending Christmas in the *Shatt-el-Arab Hotel*, Basra, as he described in his diary:[137]

I don't remember enjoying Christmas since I was a child. This Christmas Day was the worst ever. A small but virulent 'Baghdad boil' on my cheek elected to burst in the afternoon. I took to my bed and tried to sleep. The racket made rest impossible. All around was pandemonium: doors slamming, corks popping, bells ringing without being answered, hotel staff arguing, demoniac laughter echoing down the corridors. In the evening I tried to drown the pain with aspirin and went out to watch couples with glazed expressions shunting round a dance floor. Several people got drunk and were quietly removed. Returning to the Shatt-el-Arab *I found that the signs of festivity had increased. A fire-extinguisher had been let off, flooding the hall; and in the courtyard a trio of sodden soldiers were leaning into the fountain trying to catch the carp. Upstairs there was a scene of devastation. A bunch of drunken soldiers had broken into bedrooms, announcing that they were military police. Their behaviour suggested a demolition gang. My room was untouched, although those opposite and on both sides had been ransacked. Sikander, the little Chaldean Christian room-boy, told me that two soldiers had knocked down a genuine military policeman and kicked him on the head. He had been distressed to see British soldiers fighting among themselves: 'S'ils se battraient avec les arabes ce serait bien.'*[138]

---

[137] The papers of B. F. Spiller in the Imperial War Museum Documents Collection: every effort has been made to trace copyright holders and the Imperial War Museum would be grateful for any information which might help to trace those whose identities or addresses are not currently known. The *Shatt-el-Arab Hotel* is situated in northern Basra and was completed in 1937. Following the 2003 invasion of Iraq by Coalition forces, it served as an important British base, until it was handed over to the Iraqi 10th Division on 11 March 2007.
[138] 'If they fight with the Arabs that would be fine.'

On 27 December 1941 he wrote to his mother, Norah:

My life continues on the same even pattern of long office hours, interesting enough work and sometimes a bar crawl in the evening. It is discreet because of the price of drink. Actually there is a very good system of rationed whisky whereby an officer like me who doesn't live in a mess can buy a bottle of whisky on the cheap from the NAAFI if he gets there in time.[139] *A colonel told me that he always bought chocolate and found it an excellent substitute for whisky in the cold weather, but I have not had the same experience. There were turkeys for dinner at Christmas here, which I suppose there weren't at home. They were so badly cooked that there was practically no taste in them. All meat out here is pretty dull eating, because there is no proper feeding for the animals when they are alive. I don't recommend Iraq as a holiday resort.*

After serving in Egypt, North Africa, Sicily and Italy, Captain Brian Spiller's war ended with 103 Special Counter-Intelligence Unit in North-West Europe. He lived later at Wolvercote Green, near Oxford and died on 12 November 1992.

[139] NAAFI — Navy, Army and Air Force Institutes, established in 1921 to provide canteen, shopping and recreational facilities for members of the British Armed Forces.

1941/42

My wife's grandfather, Brigadier Eric Whitlock Goodman DSO MC, was Commander Royal Artillery, 9th Indian Division, which was trying to halt the inexorable Japanese advance south through the Malay Peninsula. His wartime diary begins:

I am writing up this diary as you asked in one of your letters whilst I am a POW. I started making notes for it in December last and am starting this today, the 28th July 1943. My memory is very bad now and few of the dates are accurate probably. There will also be many omissions. If you have kept my letters I should very likely be able to expand it a bit and actually I have been able to verify one or two trips I made, from your letters in answer to mine. I can at least put a great deal into this which the censor didn't allow me to put into my letters, and probably a good deal which I wrote in letters.

By Christmas, the British and Commonwealth forces were already one-third of the way down the Peninsula and the retreat was gathering pace:

In the morning back again to Kampar to see Hughes, whose HQ was installed in another of the Sultan of Perak's palaces. A dreadful place furnished in terrible, mid-Victorian style, plush curtains, masses of ornaments and terrible pictures — quite hideous . . . General Pownall, who had just taken over at GHQ Far East from Brooke-Popham, came up that day to look round and in the afternoon went up to Kampar to see the position, going up to Kampar, on to Dipang and back via Chenderiang. Between the two roads marked on the map is a hill about 3,700 feet high, so the two halves of the position were completely isolated from each other. He had tea back at Tapah and then went off . . . We had a Christmas dinner this evening, the only Christmassy thing about it being a bottle of fizz, which somebody had acquired that day from Teluk Anson.[140] It ran to about a sherry glassful each and very good it was.

[140] Now Teluk Intan, Perak, Malaysia: famous for its leaning clock-tower.

The following Christmas he was in the senior officers' prisoner-of-war camp at Karenko, in a former Presbyterian mission on the island of Formosa (now Taiwan):

Christmas with carols. A service with good singing. A loaf of bread (they tried to take our rice) and some meat in the soup, plus an orange I think.

Of that New Year's Day he wrote:

After roll call were told to give 3 banzais for the Emperor which caused some amusement and was never repeated.[141]

---

[141] Banzai – literally ten thousand years of life but, in this context, 'Long live the Emperor'.

1942

Hermione Llewellyn married Daniel Knox, 6th Earl of Ranfurly, in London on 17 January 1939. She later used their contacts to follow her husband to Egypt, where he was serving with the Nottinghamshire Yeomanry (Sherwood Rangers). After Dan was captured in April 1941, Hermione found work as PA to the High Commissioner in Palestine, Sir Harold MacMichael, and later as PA to General Sir Henry Maitland 'Jumbo' Wilson, Supreme Commander of the Mediterranean Theatre. In her wartime diaries she wrote:[142]

Yesterday was Christmas Day. When I woke I found that Freya had given me a stocking; it was filled with the few things one can get in Baghdad — poker dice, odorono, garters, a swansdown powder puff and soap in the toe.[143] *After we had waded through mud to the English church Mark, Francis and I gave a party for the orderlies and clerks in the office. I gave them all shaving brushes — the only male presents I could afford.*

Today Freya and I drove to the Palace to pay our respects to the Queen Mother. We were shown into an ornately furnished room — one seldom sees upholstered chairs or sofas in these parts because they are uncomfortable in hot weather. I had expected to meet an old lady and was surprised when the Queen walked into the room; she is about the same age as me, slight and pretty; she dresses in semi-European clothes. Freya talked to her in Arabic which I cannot understand so I sat there laughing when they laughed and shaking my head or clicking my tongue when they shook their heads or clicked their tongues. Once Freya turned to me — 'She is telling me about her son, little King Feisal [sic], who is learning

---

[142] Extract from *To War With Whitaker* by Hermione, Countess of Ranfurly (© the Estate of Hermione Ranfurly, 1994) is reproduced by kind permission of Peters Fraser & Dunlop Group Ltd, on behalf of the Estate of Hermione Ranfurly. Whitaker was Dan's butler, who also accompanied him to Egypt.

[143] Her landlady, the inveterate traveller, writer, Arabist and propagandist Freya Stark (1893–1993), was described by Hermione Ranfurly as 'a very brave lady with an iron will hidden under the hats she wears more often than not'.

English.[144] *He is only eight,' she said. I feel sorry for this charming girl who has to lead a secluded widow's life and wear nothing but black. Her husband was killed in a motor accident a few years ago; she is not allowed to marry again.*

Tonight Nigel Clive watched me while we ate dinner. His face twitched with suppressed laughter. Next time Freya left the room he said: 'I loved your 'Look out stomach — here it comes' expression. Most of the meat Jasim cooks is camel but sometimes it's cat or wild dog. The puddings aren't bad when they're not made with goat's milk . . .' Freya returned and he changed the conversation.

Dan Ranfurly escaped from his Italian prisoner-of-war camp in 1943 and he and Hermione were reunited the following year. Hermione, Countess of Ranfurly, accompanied her husband to the Bahamas, where he was Governor from 1953 to 1957. While living in Nassau she started up a local library service, which was later extended to other parts of the world short of English books, and still flourishes today as Book Aid International. Hermione Ranfurly died on 11 February 2001.

[144] Together with many other members of the ruling Hashemite family, King Faisal II was killed at the al-Zuhoor Palace, Baghdad on 14 July 1958 during a military coup.

1942

The official *History of the Second World War* matter-of-factly records the desperate struggle for Longstop Hill in Tunisia, known to the German soldiers as 'Der Weihnachtshügel', or 'Christmas Hill':[145]

On the afternoon of the 22nd it began to rain heavily. That night the 2nd Coldstream Guards overcame stiff opposition at the small railway station Halte d'el Heri but lost it to a quick counter-attack. They took Longstop Hill itself and the 1st Battalion U.S. 18th Infantry came up to replace them. The Coldstream then went back to prepare for the 1st Guards Brigade's next task. Early on the 23rd the Americans lost heavily in trying to retake the Halte, and shortly afterwards the enemy regained the top of Longstop Hill. An American counter-attack failed, whereupon Brigadier Copland-Griffiths recalled the Coldstream Guards and learnt from 5th Corps that although the main attack on Tunis had been postponed 48 hours the operation to secure Longstop Hill was to continue.[146] At about 5 p.m. on the 24th the Guards again recaptured the hill, only to realise the enemy's main positions were on Djebel el Rhaa, which they were unable to take. On Christmas morning the Germans recaptured the upper part of Longstop Hill.[147] That afternoon General Allfrey decided not to try again and ordered the operation to be broken off.[148] It had cost the Coldstream Guards 178 killed, wounded and missing and the Americans 356.

---

[145] *History of the Second World War – The Mediterranean and Middle East Volume IV*: reproduced under the terms of PSI licence number C2007001361.

[146] Brigadier Felix Copland-Griffiths, who was commanding 1st Infantry Brigade.

[147] Longstop Hill was not recaptured by the Allies, after yet more fierce fighting, until 26 April 1943.

[148] Lieutenant-General Charles Allfrey, GOC 5th Corps.

1942

General Sir Bernard Montgomery, commanding the British Eighth Army, was pushing Rommel's Deutsches Afrikakorps back across the desert towards Tripoli. In a Christmas Day letter to General Sir Alan Brooke, Chief of the Imperial General Staff, he wrote: 'Mentally, and from the point of view of morale, I think we are on top of the Bosche.' The same day he wrote to Phyllis Reynolds, guardian of his son David, thanking her for 'the lovely soft leather waistcoat you sent me'. He continued: 'I sent an ADC to Cairo to get supplies for the mess and as a result we have half a pig, six turkeys, six chickens, and various fruits and fresh vegetables. All this is very welcome as for the last month or so we have lived on biscuits and bully beef.'[149]

His opponent, Generalfeldmarschall Erwin Rommel, was neither so optimistic, nor finding life so comfortable, as he described to his wife, Lucie:[150]

Today my thoughts are more than ever with you two at home. To you, Manfred, once more all the best for your 15th year. I expect you will already have received my birthday letter.[151] And I wish you both a very happy Christmas. God will help us as in the past . . . I'm going off very early this morning into the country and will be celebrating this evening among the men. They're in top spirits, thank God, and it takes great strength not to let them see how heavily the situation is pressing on us. Kesselring was here yesterday. New promises were made, but it will be the same as it ever was. They can't be kept because the enemy puts his pencil through all our supply calculations.

[149] *Monty – Master of the Battlefield 1942–1944* by Nigel Hamilton, published by Hamish Hamilton in 1983: reproduced by kind permission of David Higham Associates.

[150] *The Rommel Papers* edited by B. H. (later Sir Basil) Liddell-Hart, published by Collins in 1953: reproduced by permission of David Higham Associates.

[151] On 6 January 1944, just nine days after his fifteenth birthday, Erwin and Lucie Rommel's only child, Manfred, was called up to serve in an anti-aircraft battery. He survived the war and held office as Christian Democrat Mayor of Stuttgart 1974–96.

In his diary Rommel wrote:

During the return journey our Christmas dinner trotted up to us in the shape of a herd of gazelles. Armbruster and I each succeeded in bringing down one of these speedy animals from the moving cars. When I arrived back at H.Q. I learnt that the British had meanwhile launched an attack south of Sirte with 4,500 vehicles and were now moving on to the west. In Sirte itself, the men of the 15th Panzer Division had just got together for their Christmas celebration when the attack came and they had to pack up and hastily evacuate the district. At about 17.00 hours General Bayerlein and I joined the H.Q. Company's Christmas party, where I received the present of a miniature petrol drum, containing, instead of petrol, a pound or two of captured coffee. Thus proper homage was paid to our most serious problem even on that day. At 20.00 hours I invited several people from my immediate staff to share a meal off the gazelles we had brought in that morning.

Implicated in the 20 July 1944 plot against Hitler, two generals visited Erwin Rommel at his home at Herrlingen – where he was convalescing after being wounded by a fighter-bomber in France – on 14 October 1944. He was offered the choice: stand trial and face charges of high treason or commit suicide. Erwin Rommel chose the latter option and died the same day, after swallowing a poison capsule.

1942

On Guadalcanal in 1942 the Japanese used Christmas cards as a psychological weapon with which they hoped to weaken the resolve of the American fighting man. A number of different cards were produced, many of them featuring pin-ups or 'Vargas' girls, as drawn by Alberto Vargas for *Esquire*. No doubt the intention was that these more than slightly suggestive images – although now appearing rather tame – would add to the appeal of the cards. Unfortunately the artist's use of Japanese models – grinning 'Geisha girls' instead of sexy 'Bunny girls' – probably amused the recipients, instead of undermining their morale. Inside the cards there is the following handwritten text:

Dearest Husband,

It's Christmas time again, and here I am, sending you my love and greetings, instead of being able to wish you the same in person. I'm sure your life is full of hardship and misery. My head aches when I wonder why we had to start this war. Oh darling, if only we could enjoy Christmas together like we used to. Remember?

Things have changed so much since you left. If you were here you wouldn't be able to believe your eyes. All the young men have gone to war. Christmas is here, but St. Nick finds us with no new hats, no cars and no silk stockings.

All of our young friends are leaving for the city in search of love and excitement. There's so much more thrill in the big cities I suppose.

Gloria and Peggy are married and both are mothers now. I wish we had a child too. I'm so lonesome. It frightens me when I think of what I'd do if I should lose you. You'll try and come back soon, won't you dear? I find it so hard waiting. Won't it be wonderful when you come back to me, whistling like you always did when you used to come home from work? Goodbye dear, take care of yourself and please hurry home.

Love and kisses,

Joan

1942

Harry Malet, a manager with Harcroft Rubber Estates at Ipoh in Malaysia, served with 4th (Pahang) Battalion, Federated Malay States Volunteer Force (FMSVF) during the Malayan campaign. When hostilities seemed likely, his wife Josephine (née Sandeman) took their four daughters – Prue, Jenny, Susan and Lindy – to Cape Town. Captain Harry Malet was captured when Singapore fell and was later sent to Kinsaiyok in Siam to work on the infamous Burma Railway. That Christmas he was at No. 3 River Camp, Kanyu and wrote in his diary:[152]

It is now 12.30 as I write and I have just come back from our Morning Service. The 'Church' – the clearing in the bamboo jungle overlooking the river – the latter flowing some 50 to 70 feet below us. The Altar is a large boulder, and behind is a bamboo cross about 5 feet tall. There must have been about 150 to 200 in Church – i.e. sitting in rows up the hillside, and Padre Parr preached quite adequately. At 8.30 I went to Holy Communion at which there were over 100 Communicants and very beautiful it was. The early sun coming through the morning mist and shining on the river and opposite jungle-clad hills – the real time being 6.30 of course. The early bird songs in the trees around us and the old accustomed monkey calls 'Wah-Wah's' being the most prevalent. A small flight of giant toucans flew over and the wild peacocks called to each other stridently – as I say – a really jungle setting for our Christmas Communion, with the 14 little white crosses of our cemetery beside us. As we waited for the Service to begin – sitting on split bamboos on the ground – I worked out that Jo was then at that moment probably coming home from Midnight Mass in the glorious full moonlight.

At midnight last night I went to Mass – in the R.C. 'Church' – a little clearing in the bamboo jungle on the hillside between the two valleys in which our huts are built. They have a little Altar,

[152] The papers of Captain H. F. G. Malet in the Imperial War Museum Documents Collection, by kind permission of Mrs Susan Tanner.

Altar rails and side table — all fronted with ataps.[153] *Candles in bamboo sconces were lighted — incense made from jungle dammar was duly swung in a censer made from an old jam tin burnished and hung on an old dog chain, but the whole effect was perfect!*[153] *. . . Father Burke gave a delightful address on the subject of our Homes and Loved Ones and, of course, my object in going was chiefly to feel I was sharing (in such amazingly different surroundings) in just such a Service as my own little family are going to, or at any rate Jo will be going if she is able. This time last year we were in bivouacs in the jungle at Kemubu having just withdrawn to a defended position south of the river. I was talking to Al Hazlett after breakfast and reminding him of last Xmas when a voice came from behind us saying, 'Yes, I was there too!' It was Capt Edgar of the R.E.s — just emerged from 2 weeks in hospital with dysentery. I had not met him since Singapore before the Capitulation (another Old Cheltonian — making about half a dozen or more in this Camp!).*[155]

December 26th — Boxing Day

Yesterday we had a disappointment as our Xmas Dinner — one pig — was found to be alive with maggots and quite unfit for consumption! We had a 'pasty' made of sweet potato with our usual root jungle stew. From the canteen 5/- allowance we opened a tin of ovals between the three of us — Geoff Brown, Leslie Jerram and myself. That gave us 3½ sardines each, which added to the rice, pasty and stew, gave us our Christmas dinner — and very nice too. We are not accustomed to such richness and went to bed feeling absolutely bloated. What worries us is to think how incapable we shall be of doing justice to a real Xmas Dinner next year if we can't deal with this one.

Captain Harry Malet never 'did justice' to another Christmas dinner: he died at Kanyu on 4 June 1943 and is buried in Kanchanaburi War Cemetery, Thailand. His diary was returned to his wife after the war by a family friend, Dr Robert Hardie, who also served in the

[153] Ataps — palm-leaf thatch.

[154] Dammar — gum obtained from local trees.

[155] Harry Malet attended Cheltenham College, making him an Old Cheltonian. Traditional British loyalties survived the barbaric treatment of the Japanese. Eric Goodman (see 1941/42) wrote: 'We had an OW [Old Wellingtonian] dinner on June 18th, everyone contributing something in the way of food. There were 30 odd.' 18 June is the anniversary of the battle of Waterloo.

FMSVF.[156] Jo Malet never remarried but returned to England and, finding it hard to manage on a very modest Army pension, took in children whose parents lived abroad and who could not return home for the school holidays.

[156] See *The Burma-Siam Railway – The secret diary of Dr. Robert Hardie 1942–45*, published by the Imperial War Museum in 1983: '22 February 1945 – Harry Malet's diary, which he kept up at Kanyu in 1943, has come into my hands. It ends in April 1943, shortly before he died. His diary shows clearly the awful shortage of supplies – and that, when canteen supplies came in, the Japanese seized the occasion or excuse to cut down the ration issues still more. Harry kept fit until near the end, but had to work terribly hard. The Jap camp commandant at Kanyu openly admitted that the general in charge of the railway had said that he did not mind what happened to the prisoners – the railway must go through as fast as possible. Harry finally died, quite quickly, of dysentery and malaria. It is pathetic to read his constant thoughts of his family.'

1942

James Lees-Milne, prolific author and diarist, was born in 1908, the son of a 'philistine fox-hunting father', whose wishes he wilfully denied 'by parading an assumed dilettantism and aestheticism'. In 1940 he joined the Irish Guards but, diagnosed with Jacksonian epilepsy, was invalided out in late 1941. On Christmas Eve he wrote in his diary:[157]

I went home for Christmas, or rather I stayed with Midi in the village, having half my meals with her and half with the family. Midi's younger child Veronica is undeniably beautiful with copper-coloured hair and a fair skin, but she tries to be funny, and is strikingly unfunny. Bamber is a sensitive, delicate and adventurous little boy.[158] Deenie has come down from Stowe for Christmas.[159] She is very miserable because one of her two great friends is dying, and she regrettably made a deathbed promise that she would have the surviving friend to live with her for the rest of her days, a rash thing to do. And so I told her.

Mama told me how last week she was in the room while Papa and Colonel Riley were planning a Home Guard exercise to take place the following day. Rather brutally they intended to humiliate another officer for stupidity, saying to each other, 'William, the damned fool, will never be able to capture the aerodrome. If he were the slightest use, of course he would, etc.' They then discussed how it ought to be done, tracing on a map the complicated route he should take, mentioning the names of bridges, roads, villages and the map numbers. Mama all the while was pretending to read The Times, *but was actually jotting down on a pad all they said. When they left the house she rang up the damned fool William, and reported to him word for word what they had said, giving the exact map references. The result was that much to their surprise and disgust William captured the aerodrome with flying colours. When I told Midi this she said, 'Your mother told me in*

---

[157] *Ancestral Voices*, published by Chatto & Windus in 1975: reproduced by permission of David Higham Associates.
[158] The Hon Mary O'Neill, (Midi), was married to Derek Gascoigne, and her two children, Bamber, the author and broadcaster, and Veronica.
[159] Doreen Cuninghame, his mother's widowed sister.

confidence that whenever she wants to get out of the Red Cross functions she puts her thermometer on the hot-water bottle, and shows it to your father, who positively forbids her to leave her bed. Your mother, to make her feigned illness more convincing expostulates with your father just a little, but not too much, knowing that he will not give his consent.'

In 1936 he joined The National Trust, serving as adviser on historic buildings from 1951 until his retirement in 1966. James Lees-Milne died on 28 December 1997.

1942

In retaliation for the internment in 1941 of German citizens living in Iran, Hitler ordered that more than 2,000 British-born inhabitants of the Channel Islands should be removed from their homes and interned in Germany. Accompanied by her parents, Frank and Annie, and her sister, Beryl, thirty year-old Joan Salmon left Jersey for St. Malo on 18 September 1942. A group of 618 internees finally arrived at the Schloß at Bad Wurzach in south-eastern Baden-Württemberg on 31 October. That Christmas Joan Salmon wrote in her diary:[160]

We awoke at 5.30 this Xmas morn to hear the first of 19 children discovering what Father Christmas had put into their small stockings! Gradually the voices rose to a crescendo until all 19 children were laughing and talking at once. Fragments from Red Cross parcels, bits of material made into quaint animals and numerous little wooden toys, all made in the camp, helped to make this day as happy as possible for the children. All rooms were gaily decorated with crepe paper, chains and bright festoons, mostly obtained from Red Cross parcels, & some had been passed in by the 'G' guards. Christmas trees were brought in from the village and placed in the larger rooms, where they were later trimmed with small gifts of chocolate, cigarettes, and hand-made articles.

A Holy Communion service was held on Xmas Eve, with a good attendance. The necessary articles for this service were kindly provided by the visiting R.C. priest as also was the beautifully adorned crib and Holy Child, which was placed on the simple wooden altar. This was complete with hand embroidered altar linen and exquisite vessels for the Sacraments. The Reverend Atyeo officiated and 40–50 internees partook of Holy Communion many miles from their homes & families.[161]

---

[160] The papers of Mrs J. Coles in the Imperial War Museum Documents Collection: every effort has been made to trace copyright holders and the Imperial War Museum would be grateful for any information which might help to trace those whose identities or addresses are not currently known.

[161] The Reverend Cecil Bingham Atyeo, who died on 27 February 1945, aged sixty-two.

A Special Menu was supplied by the Chef and his colleagues, consisting of: *La Crème Bons Voeux; Le Boeuf Braisé de Rois Mages; Les Choise son Façons; Les Pommes Sautée à la Schloss; Le Plum Pudding; Merci Croix Rouge; Le Thé soient Benes Les Marins Britanniques*. Beer was on draught for all men and women over 21 and payable in Camp money.

A Children's Party was held in the Theatre from 2—4.30. Father Xmas was present and gave each child a packet of sweets. Prizes, supplied by the Red Cross, were given for various competitions. Bread and Butter, Cake and Tea at 4.30!

In room 70 preparations for a dinner party of 21 persons continued until 7.30 when we all sat down to another excellent Red Cross repast. Captain and Mrs. Hilton graced the head of the table and the various families sat the full length of the table. This was gaily decorated with our National Colours, complete with flowers (paper) and a small Xmas tree laden with small gifts of sweets and cigarettes. Toasts to our King, the Ladies and the International Red Cross were interspersed with song, until our table was stripped of all its good things. During the evening a large throng of people marched the corridors, singing popular songs, some old, some new. In the Main Entrance Hall several solos were beautifully rendered including Queen Elizabeth's famous song from 'Merry England'. After a few games in our room, we retired to bed at 11.55 feeling well fed but rather tired after our first (and last Xmas Day, we hope!) Christmas behind barbed wire.

Two more, increasingly austere, Christmases had to be endured before the internees were eventually liberated by the French Army on 28 April 1945. In 1974 Mrs Joan Coles (née Salmon) wrote: 'Three years ago a small party of Internees returned to the Castle and were given a very warm welcome by the Mayor, Herr Hirth and last year a party of about thirty people returned again for a week's celebrations, this time the village was celebrating 500 years of its history and felt that as we had been part of that history, some Internees should be their guests. For several years now there has been an exchange of school children each summer and so we feel we are offering the hand of friendship where once there was hatred.' Joan Coles died in 1997.

1942

Ralph and Frances Partridge lived at Ham Spray House in Wiltshire. Having served as an infantry officer during the First World War, twice being awarded the Military Cross, Ralph registered as a Conscientious Objector at the start of the Second World War. Frances Partridge wrote in her diary on 29 December:[162]

Christmas is over at last. We were over twenty to see Professor Frisco's conjuring display. His personality was most sympathetic, and the things he produced from his hat or tambourines were ravishingly pretty — huge bright handkerchiefs folding to nothing, palm trees of coloured feathers. The tea-table was piled with cakes and jellies and the tree had a proper present for each child. It was much enjoyed and Burgo thanked me formally: 'I do really congratulate you.'[163] But of course the whole occasion was made for me unreal and dreamlike by the fact that R. set off to his tribunal at early dawn and didn't return till the guests had departed. I couldn't get over the queerness of our experiencing such very different days.

As he came up the stairs he said, 'No luck at all.' He told me he had gone there full of belief in British justice, and the conviction that since his pacifism is sincere the judges were sure to discover the fact. I was rather surprised that he hadn't anticipated, as I had, the hostile and angry light in which they would view him. We have had ample proof (for instance Gerald's violent reaction) of what emotion is aroused by disagreement on this subject.[164] Anxious not to get angry, he had remained uncharacteristically meek while they lectured him about the Treaty of Versailles, told him as sympathetically as they were able that he was a war-weary veteran of the last war, and made no attempt to question him about his views whatever. The proceedings lasted ten minutes; the Tribunal's findings were 'we are not satisfied that there is a conscientious objection within the

[162] Extract from *A Pacifist's War*, published by Hogarth Press in 1978 (© the Estate of Frances Partridge) is reproduced by permission of Rogers, Coleridge & White Ltd, 20 Powis Mews, London W11 1JN.

[163] Ralph and Frances Partridge's only son, then aged 7. He died of a heart attack at the age of 28.

[164] Their great friend Gerald Brenan, a distinguished hispanophile.

meaning of the act in this case,' and 'that the applicant's name be removed from the Register of Conscientious Objectors'. He came away thoroughly frustrated. The facts came out at once, his emotional reaction only gradually, and of course he spent a wretched night thinking of all the things he ought to have said. How I wish we had discussed it more, and rehearsed the statements, that he must get out whatever questions the judges asked. We had buried our heads in the sand, like ostriches. He is going to write to Craig Macfarlane to ask if it is possible to appeal, and whether it would be a good thing to get letters testifying to the sincerity of his views.

On 9 March 1943 Ralph Partridge made a successful appeal to the Tribunal. Often described as the last survivor of the 'Bloomsbury Group', Frances Partridge died on 5 February 2004, at the age of one hundred and three.

1943

When Adolf Hitler came to power in 1933, Otto and Edith Frank moved – with their daughters Margot and Anne – from Frankfurt to Amsterdam, where Otto set up the Dutch branch of the family company, Opekta, a pectin manufacturer. On 5 July 1942 Margot Frank received a call-up notice from the SS and Otto decided that the family, together with four friends, should go into hiding in the so-called Secret Annexe at 263 Prinsengracht, Amsterdam. On 27 December 1943 fourteen year-old Anne Frank wrote in her diary:[165]

Friday evening, for the first time in my life, I received a Christmas present. Mr Kleiman, Mr Kugler and the girls had prepared a wonderful surprise for us. Miep made a delicious Christmas cake with 'Peace 1944' written on top, and Bep provided biscuits that were up to pre-war standards. There was a pot of yoghurt for Peter, Margot and me, and a bottle of beer for each of the adults.[166] And once again everything was wrapped so nicely, with pretty pictures glued to the parcels. For the rest, the holidays passed by quickly for us.

On the morning of 4 August 1944 a car pulled up outside 263 Prinsengracht and an SS sergeant and at least three Dutch members of the Security Police got out. They arrested the eight occupants of the Secret Annexe, together with two of their helpers, Johannes Kleiman and Victor Kugler. While the latter two survived, only one of those hiding in the Secret Annexe remained alive at the end of the war: Otto

---

[165] From *The Diary of a Young Girl – The Definitive Edition*, Otto H. Frank and Miriam Pressler, Editors, translated by Susan Massotty, copyright © 1995 by Doubleday, a division of Bantam Doubleday Dell Publishing Group Inc, 1995: reproduced by permission of Penguin Books Ltd.
[166] Peter van Pels, seventeen year-old son of Hermann and Auguste van Pels from Osnabrück, Germany, Otto Frank's business partner. This family of three were in the Annexe, together with Dr. Fritz Pfeffer, a dentist from Giessen. Just one in sixteen of Amsterdam's Jewish population survived the war.

Frank. Anne Frank died of typhus, a few days after her sister, at Bergen-Belsen in late February or early March 1945. The British Army liberated the camp on 12 April 1945.

Neither of the two secretaries who worked for Opekta – Miep Gies or Elisabeth (Bep) Voskuijl – was arrested. After the police departed, Miep and Bep found Anne's diaries scattered all over the floor and Miep placed them in a drawer for safe-keeping. After the war Otto Frank returned to Amsterdam from Auschwitz-Birkenau, where his wife had died on 6 January 1945, travelling via Odessa and Marseilles and arriving on 3 June 1945. He first published edited excerpts from his daughter's diary in 1947, remarried, moved to Birsfelden, near Basle in 1953 and died there on 19 August 1980, having devoted the rest of his life to Anne Frank's memory.

1943

Madame Anne Brusselmans, who was half-English, was a member of the Comet Line (Comète) and lived with her husband, Julien, and their two children, Yvonne and Jacques, in a flat above a gas showroom in Brussels. Comète helped to pass downed Allied airman along a complex chain from Brussels, through occupied France via Paris by train, and then across the Pyrénées to San Sebastian in neutral Spain, and finally to Gibraltar and back to Britain. She was engaged in her vital, but hazardous, task at Christmas 1943:[167]

Before leaving with the two men for the station I had to buy a suit for Bud, and what a job it was. Why are those Americans so tall? It is so hard to find clothes to fit them. As for getting ten men like this one into a B17 it looks to me that they must have to be folded in half before entering the 'plane. Yet they say they are very comfortable inside. The usual preparations begin as the time approaches for them to leave. First, I see that all their identity discs (or dog tags as they call them) are securely in their clothes, for if they are caught they must be able to prove they are airmen trying to escape and are not spies. Lorne has a cigarette-lighter which his mother gave him as a 21st birthday present. It has his name and address on it, so we will have to find a safe place to hide this for he won't leave it behind. These men are superstitious about such things — a feeling I know well . . .

Before the men left they helped me make a Christmas tree but we are running out of decorations for it. However, the bombers drop a lot of aluminium strips to jam the German radar screen, and we are making do with this for decorating the tree. This is our fourth war Christmas and the children won't believe us now when we tell them it will be the last one. I have been going round the shops to see if I can find a few toys for Jacques. He is eight years old. Yvonne is twelve, and she has to understand it is impossible to give her Christmas presents. She is very reasonable about

---

[167] *Rendez-Vous 127* by Anne Brusselmans, published by Ernest Benn in 1954: reprinted by kind permission of Yvonne Daley Brusselmans.

this and it makes it easier for us to tell her, but it squashes any hope she may have had. After visiting all the shops, all I could find were a few tin soldiers dressed in German uniforms, or German tanks, and German machine-guns, all marked with the iron cross and swastika. I just will not give such toys as these to my son to play with. I would rather see him disappointed once more. But I have made up my mind that when this war is ended he and Yvonne will have all the toys they long for, even if it means I have to work until the end of my life to get them. And so another Christmas day comes and passes in wartime. I hope it is the last one.

More than 750 Allies reached freedom through Comète but the cost was high: among other losses, eleven members of Comète were executed by firing squad on 20 October 1943.[168] For her war services Anne Brusselmans was awarded the Belgian Croix de Guerre with silver palm, was made a Member of the British Empire and also received the Presidential Medal of Freedom, the highest US civilian award. President Ronald Reagan made her a permanent resident of the United States in 1987 and, as a result, she was reunited, during the last six years of her life, with several of the US airman to whom she had given assistance during the war.

[168] There is a window to Comète in the RAF Chapel in the National Basilica, Koekelberg, Belgium.

1943

General Sir Bernard Montgomery, commanding the Eighth Army in Italy, sent a 'Personal Message from the Army Commander (To be read out to all Troops)':

1. Once again the Eighth Army spends Christmas in the field. This time last year we were in Tripolitania, having just broken through the famous Agheila position; now, we are well north of an east and west line through Rome. And I would say to you, soldiers of the Eighth Army, that you have every right to be very proud of what you have achieved during the past year; every officer and man has done his duty in a manner that is beyond all praise.

2. And so this Christmas, 1943, I send to every officer and man in the great family of the Eighth Army, my best wishes and hearty greetings. And I send greetings from us all to your loved ones and friends in your homelands; they are, indirectly, part of this great Army in that their courage and fortitude is essential to the morale of the Army itself. And I know that you will wish me to send our greetings also to all the workers on the home front; without their hard work in the factories and mines, we could win no victories in the field.

3. And today we recall the Christmas message:

> *GLORY TO GOD IN THE HIGHEST, AND ON EARTH*
> *PEACE, GOODWILL TOWARD MEN.*

Surely this describes exactly what we are fighting for? Let us, therefore, take it as our battle cry and our motto; and in doing so let us affirm that between us, you and I, we will see this thing through to the end.

4. And when peace has come, I like to think that the spirit of the Eighth Army will be a factor for good in the unsettled and difficult days that will lie ahead. Wherein lies the strength of this great

Army? It lies in its team spirit, in the firm determination of every man to do his duty, and in its high morale. This Army is a great family, with an ARMY 'esprit de corps' and spirit the like of which can seldom have been seen before. When war is over and we all scatter to our various tasks, let us see to it that the spirit of the Eighth Army lives on; may it be a great and powerful influence in the re-building of the nations. The Christmas message will be our battle cry, not only now, but also in the years to come.

5. A Happy Christmas to you all and to your families wherever they may be.

Just six days later Montgomery gave up command of the Eighth Army and returned to England to prepare for Operation *Overlord*, the D-Day landings.

1943

Lance-Bombardier Terence Alan 'Spike' Milligan was serving in Italy with 19th Battery, 56th Heavy Regiment, Royal Artillery. He wrote:[169]

'Looking forward to Christmas, Harry?' Edgington looks up from his mess-tin. 'I'm not sure, mate, in one way yes, in another no, the no part is spending it away from home. You can't help feeling homesick, and it's worse at Christmas.'

There is no place to be at Christmas except home. I thought of the Christmasses I remembered from boyhood days in Poona. I remember the little room I slept in at the back of the house in 5 Climo Road, the indescribable excitement of waking at four in the morning, with the world of adults all silent, finding the pillow-case full of boxes and toys, and the magic as you unwrapped each one . . . I remember waking up at the very moment my mother and grandmother were putting the pillow-case at the bottom of my bed, explaining how 'Father Christmas had just gone', and when I asked which way he went, they pointed at the window; as it was covered with chicken wire, I worked out that he was magic, had got through the holes and was now a jig-saw puzzle. All that and more was moving in the memory bank of my past, and I too knew that Christmas on a farm in Italy could never be the real thing . . .

Like a jig-saw puzzle we all fit into place around the table. We sat on an assortment of chairs, stools, tins, logs. We are served, as is the tradition of the Royal Artillery, by the Officers and Sergeants. Lieutenant Walker is the wine waiter; himself having partaken of several pre-lunch drinks he is missing the glasses by a substantial amount. Gunner Musclewhite has a lapful of white Chianti, and Gunner Bailey is getting red wine among his greens. The Sergeants are ladelling out tinned turkey, pork, beef, roast vegetables, sprouts, carrots and gravy. None of our 'waiters' are quite sober and there is an overlap at the end of the dinner when Sgt. Ryan is pouring custard over

[169] *Mussolini – His Part In My Downfall*, published by Michael Joseph in 1978: reproduced by permission of Spike Milligan Productions Limited. On 20 January 1944 Spike Milligan was wounded and, suffering from what we now call Post-Traumatic Stress Disorder, sent to hospital in Caserta. No longer fit for active service, he joined ENSA, or Entertainments National Service Association, affectionately known as 'Every Night Something Awful'.

the turkey. As the wine takes effect, the chatter and laughter increase. For duff we have Christmas pudding and custard.

''Urry up, you buggers', said Sgt. 'Daddy' Wilson, 'we're waitin' to 'ave ours.' There seemed endless helpings and unlimited supplies of red and white wine, but it was a long way from the Dickensian Christmas around a log fire in the parlour, with Grandma and Grandpa present. However, when you are pissed, all that nostalgia goes out the window.

1943

After bitter fighting at Monte Cassino, twenty-four year-old Fusilier Glyn Edwards, 8th Battalion, Royal Fusiliers, celebrated a late Christmas in the village of Casanova. On 3 January 1944 he wrote to his parents, William and Blodwyn:[170]

These few lines to let you know I am still alive and well . . . I have not been able to write for a couple of weeks now, as you may guess where I've been, but now we are back for a rest for a few days and, believe me Mam, we need it, as we had such terrible weather while in the line. How is Dad these days? Is he still working regular and I suppose is still in the Home Guard and doing his soldiering. I wish I was in that mob. We are having our Christmas day tomorrow 4 January, as we were in an awkward spot for Dec. 25th, but it really doesn't matter what day we have it out here, as every day is the same now: I hope you had a good Xmas at home, I hope to be with you for next year, as I hope to God that 1944 will see it all over with, and that I am away from stinking Italy . . . While we were down in the line it rained continuously . . . I'm feeling quite fit since I've been here, Mam (despite the conditions I have had plenty of oranges and other fruit. I suppose I shall get sick of them soon). I am getting to pick this language up OK now. You should hear me and one of these Italians in conversation, it's a scream to see.

Glyn Edwards was killed in action at Anzio on 24 February 1944. Second Lieutenant Eric Waters, father of *Pink Floyd* lyricist, Roger Waters, served in the same battalion and was killed the same week. His son, only five months old at the time, subsequently wrote a sardonic tribute song, 'When the Tigers Broke Free'.

[170-] *Monte Cassino* by Matthew Parker, published by Headline in 2003: reprinted by kind permission of Headline Publishing Group Ltd.

1943

On the night of 11/12 August 1942 Eric Newby took part in Operation *Whynot*, a Special Boat Service raid on the airfield at Gela, Sicily. The whole raiding party was captured. On 9 September the following year, despite a broken ankle, he took advantage of the confusion surrounding the Italian Armistice to escape from the prison hospital at Fontanellato, near Parma, assisted by Wanda Skof and her father. That Christmas he was still on the run in the Apennines with a fellow escapee:[171]

On Christmas Eve we were invited to go down to the village where we spent the evening and the next day as the guests of various families, including that of Amadeo and of the man who had mended my boot. 'What would you like more than anything?' a little signora said on Christmas Eve, while her children looked up wide-eyed at these strange, smoke-stained visitors from another world. It was her husband who had helped to build our beds in the barn. There was no doubt about what we would like most, either in my mind or in James's. Although we had got ourselves as clean as possible by washing in the icy spring beneath the barn, what we both wanted more than anything was a hot bath. 'And you shall have it,' she said. Soon she had a number of enormous vessels heating on the wood stove and another, even bigger one, over the fire. And when the water was hot she half-filled a big empty wine barrel in the cellar next door. We stripped off by turns — it was no time for false modesty — and because the barrel was too close a fit for either of us to move our arms, she and her husband took turns to scrub us and wash our hair.

On Christmas Day, after a great lunch, we were taken to the house of an engineer who was in charge of the hydro-electric works on the mountain and there, at three o'clock, to the accompaniment of awful whistlings and other atmospherics, we heard the laboured but sincere-sounding voice of the King speaking from Sandringham. 'Some of you may hear me in your

[171] *Love and War in the Apennines*, published by Hodder and Stoughton in 1971: reproduced by permission of HarperCollins Publishers Ltd. © 1971 Eric Newby.

aircraft, in the jungles of the Pacific or on the Italian Peaks,' he said. 'Wherever you may be your thoughts will be in distant places and your hearts with those you love.' And although it was almost certainly not intended for people like us, the effect of what he said was too much in conjunction with all the food we had eaten and the wine we had drunk, and the people in the room witnessed the awful spectacle, something which they are unlikely ever to see again, of two Englishmen with tears running down their cheeks. And late that evening I received a little strip of paper with only two words on it — Baci, Wanda.[172] It was the best Christmas I had ever had.

Four days later Eric Newby was recaptured and spent the rest of the war in prisoner-of-war camps. After the war, having been awarded the Military Cross for his part in Operation *Whynot*, he returned to Italy to find Wanda. They were married at the church of Santa Croce in Florence in April 1946. He later became a distinguished travel writer — *The Last Grain Race*, *A Short Walk in the Hindu Kush*, *Slowly Down the Ganges* — and died on 20 October 2006.

---

[172] Baci — Italian for kisses.

1943

In 1943 Alfred de Grazia, all of whose grandparents were of Sicilian extraction, was serving with the US Army in Italy. Only in his early twenties, his views were nevertheless highly valued and he advised on the bombing of the Abbey at Monte Cassino, on the liberation of Rome and the structure of the new government and on the introduction of Italian troops into the Allied front line, before ending his brief military career as head of psychological warfare for the US Seventh Army. His wartime correspondence with his wife Jill comprises some 775,000 words. That Christmas she wrote to him:[173]

Darling — Tuesday

I've already written you a fairly long Air Mail letter earlier this evening. But not trusting any form of mail these days, and wanting to talk to you anyway, I'll put off bedtime a little longer. I had some sewing to do tonight & tried to lighten the hateful task by listening to the radio, which dripped Xmas cheer all over the rug. As a result, I am cheerless in the exact proportions to which Bob Hope et al were full of holiday mirth. There is a peculiar psychology in missing someone you love — the pain becomes greatest during the times you deviate from the ordinary, & to most people, distasteful, routine of living — the Sundays, the feast days, the idle moments just before you go to bed. Last Christmas seemed incomplete because we had to spend it in an unfamiliar clime, away from any of our families. How ungrateful I was! This Christmas there'll be the family, but no you — an infinitely less desirable state of affairs, even though I'll have the enviable role of playing Momma & hostess to the folks, because they'll be coming down here for dinner. But I almost wish the baby would start coming Christmas Eve, so I could be preoccupied and therefore spared these poignant thoughts of you on Christmas Day. However, I'm not forgetting that the pain I feel for

---

[173] *Home Front and War Front in WWII: The Correspondence of Alfred de Grazia and Jill Oppenheim de Grazia*, published by Metron Publications in 1998: reproduced by kind permission of Alfred de Grazia.

your absence is yours many times over, since your Christmas has all the disadvantages — a strange country, no family, no Jill, and a natural apprehension about the baby.[174] *I almost wish you could have the baby (painlessly) so you wouldn't have to worry about me. It would be pleasant, anyway, to see the consternation of 5th Army medics if that were to happen.*

Stay healthy, dear one

All my love,

Jill

Among many academic distinctions, Alfred de Grazia was Professor of Social Theory at New York University from 1959 to 1977.

---

[174] Now Dr Catherine de Grazia Vanderpool, President of the Board of the Gennadius Library, American School of Classical Studies, Athens.

1943

Iris, only daughter of William Bayard Cutting Jr., and grand-daughter of the last Earl and Countess of Desart, lived with her mother for fourteen years in the *Villa Medici* at Fiesole, near Florence before marrying Antonio Origo and buying a farm in southern Tuscany. They had two young daughters, Benedetta and Donata, and by Christmas the war was beginning to lap their shores and threaten the family:[175]

The Pope's Christmas Eve homily had a despairing ring, as if he himself knew all too well that his appeal for peace to men of goodwill would fall upon ears deaf to any interpretation of right and justice but their own. Almost desperate, too, was his appeal for better international understanding, based on a universal human solidarity. But indeed of this has there been (certainly here, and I believe almost everywhere) a reawakening. In church this morning as I looked round I saw, among the usual Christmas congregation from the farms and the fattoria, *the large group of refugee children from Genoa and Turin, rosy-cheeked and plump and excited; the Calabrian and Sicilian soldiers who are working in the farms; the Egyptian boy from the G.I.L.E.; all those who have found refuge here — and coming out I felt, in the familiar exchange of Christmas greetings, a bond of deep understanding born of common trouble, anxieties and hopes such as I never have felt before. And in the attitude of the farmers to all the homeless passers-by (whether Italian soldiers or British prisoners, whether Gentile or Jew) there is a spontaneous, unfailing charity and hospitality. Even now that the risks have increased — since the police are supposed to be rounding up the boys of the 1925 class — there is no farm which would refuse them shelter; and to-day I noticed that each one of the soldiers who are living here was wearing at least one garment given off their backs by their hosts.*

Yesterday we took a small Christmas tree to the Montepulciano hospital for sick children; to-day we had a tree and a party for Benedetta and the refugee children here. The older girls danced

[175] *War in the Val d'Orcia* by Iris Origo, published by Jonathan Cape in 1947: reprinted by arrangement with Allison and Busby Ltd. Text copyright © Iris Origo, 1947.

and recited, they all sang Stille Nacht *and* Tu scendi dalle stelle — *and Antonio made a magnificent Father Christmas with a flowing white beard, fur coat and cossack cap. For an hour or so it seemed like any other Christmas. But then the telephone rang: the Chianciano policeman issued a warning that Adino must report himself to-morrow morning, or the police would come to arrest his father, Gigi.*[176] *Adino promptly disappears.*

Turning on the radio in the evening, we hear of the bombing of Pistoia and Pisa.

The Origos left *La Foce* for Montepulciano on 22 June 1944; the Scots Guards arrived a week later.

---

[176] Gigi, the gardener at *La Foce*, was the only casualty in the Origo family circle, being killed by shellfire.

1943

Joseph Hirsh was from a Jewish family in Bethnal Green in the East End of London. Having begun his architectural studies at the Northern Polytechnic in London, he joined the Royal Corps of Signals, was posted to 18th British Division and 'was put in the bag' on 15 February 1942, just days after disembarking at Singapore. He was a prisoner of war for the next three-and-a-half years, 'mostly working on the notorious railway'. At Christmas 1943 he was in the Northern Siamese jungle camp of Tampin and kept the menu of that Christmas dinner as a memento. The fare was:[177]

Fish Savoury

Sausage and Eggs
Stuffed Marrow
Paloney

Lime Pudding
Sauce

Xmas Cake

Coffee and Biscuits

---

[177] In a letter dated 28 March 2007, he wrote: 'My memory of Christmas '43 is very vague. I cannot remember eating such a meal. I suppose we may have had all those items but I am inclined to think there was an element of wishful thinking and some, if not all, were mostly made of rice.'

On Thursday 16 August 1945 he wrote in his diary:[178]

I cannot hope to give an adequate description of the overwhelming emotional feeling of the day. We were released from our slavery. For 3½ years we have suffered, slaved, seen so many comrades die & endured the pitiless tyranny of the Japanese. All through the dark days the only thing that kept us going was the hope that one day we would be free, but when? — when? Our minds were fixed on some dim dreamlike future day, that ever receded from us when we seemed to approach it, like a wall of mist.

After the war Joe Hirsh resumed his architectural studies, qualifying in 1947 and eventually becoming the Divisional Planning Officer for Central London. Following a local Government reorganisation in 1965, he set up the new Planning Department for the City of Westminster. He was awarded the CBE in 1978 and retired a year later.

[178] The papers of Joseph Hirsh Esq CBE in the Imperial War Museum Documents Collection: by kind permission of Joseph Hirsh.

1943

The first major Allied victory in the West came with the surrender of more than 275,000 members of the Deutsches Afrikakorps in Tunis on 13 May 1943. They had to be accommodated somewhere and some were sent to Camp Ruston in Louisiana. A purpose-built facility, spread over 770 acres, it could hold 4,315 prisoners-of-war. One of them, Hans S. Kaiser, wrote:[179]

To my loved ones at home!

We celebrated Christmas again, and again I am not with you. But that's only the outside appearance. All my thoughts belong to you and therefore you are with me as well. I still did not get mail from you so all there is is the worries about you. I am doing very good. We started Christmas Eve with a church service. Then we had the celebration. The Führer gave all of us a money gift. We received 88 German cigarettes, tobacco, and cookies from the Red Cross. We really appreciate it. We know that home won't forget the sons and we won't forget home. Our thoughts are with you, the Führer and all our comrades at the front lines. Yesterday we had church service again. We spend time playing cards and telling stories. Today in the afternoon there is a soccer game and tonight there will be a concert. I wonder if this Christmas was the last one in war? To my loved ones I send a thousand greetings.

Yours,

Hans

A lengthy incarceration led to the development of lasting friendships, not only between the prisoners themselves, but also between the

[179] The Camp Ruston Foundation, Inc.

prisoners and their guards. For example, Otto Fernholz of Hagen enjoyed a long correspondence with Vince Spione, President of the Camp Ruston Foundation. In December 1992 Otto was planning to visit Camp Ruston with his wife Ursula for the 50th Anniversary, but his fellow POWs did not react 'with much enthusiasm'. He went on: 'I think there is a money question for most of them, and perhaps getting older also matters'. He ended the letter by wishing 'a merry Christmas and a happy and healthy New Year 1993 to you and your family'.

1944

The so-called Battle of the Bulge was the last throw of the dice for the German armies on the Western Front. The German strategic reserve was used for one final push, which caught the Americans by surprise in what had been regarded as a quiet sector. Once again, propaganda was used in an attempt to undermine morale. The Germans dropped leaflets with Christmas symbols, and the following text, on soldiers of the US 101st Airborne Division, besieged in the Belgian town of Bastogne:

Well soldier here you are in 'No-Mans-Land', just before Christmas far away from home and your loved ones. Your sweetheart or wife, your little girl, or perhaps even your little boy, don't you feel them worrying about you, praying for you? Yes old boy, praying and hoping you'll come home again, soon. Will you come back, are you sure to see those dear ones again?

This is Christmas-time, Yule-tide, the Yule-log, the Mistletoe, the Christmas-tree, whatever it is it's home and all that you think fine to celebrate the day of our Saviour. Man, have you thought about it, what if you don't come back, what of those dear ones?

Well soldier, 'PEACE ON EARTH GOOD WILL TOWARDS MEN' . . . for where there's a will there's a way . . . only 100 yards ahead and . . . MERRY CHRISTMAS!

On Thursday 22 December General von Lüttwitz of XLVII Panzer Corps sent four emissaries to deliver a message inviting surrender 'To the USA Commander of the encircled town of Bastogne'. Having reached the American lines at 11.30 a.m. they were blindfolded and taken to the command post of 327th Infantry Company. The message was then delivered to the acting Divisional Chief of Staff, Lieutenant-Colonel Ned Moore, who duly informed Brigadier-General Tony McAuliffe, acting Divisional Commander. The Germans insisted on a written reply and that from General McAuliffe has since passed into legend, as well as being perhaps the shortest entry in *The Oxford Dictionary of Quotations*: 'Nuts!' Somewhat puzzled, the leading German spokesman asked: 'Is the reply negative or affirmative?'

In Bastogne today the Historical Center is known affectionately as Nuts Museum, there is a Nuts Café serving *Nuts Salade* while many of the shops in the town sell merchandise – T-shirts and coffee mugs, etc. – emblazoned with the word 'Nuts'.

1944

Despite the war, the Second Household Cavalry Regiment managed to find the time to celebrate Christmas in Belgium:[180]

Meanwhile those of us not on duty soon found excuses to borrow a vehicle and pay calls on neighbours along the river bank. On the road from Tirlemont to Diest, Major Williams's Headquarter Squadron was billeted in the village of Bunsbeek, as were most of the Squadron echelons. The houses were most adequate and the people, as usual, extremely hospitable. Lieutenants Oliver (when he was not in Brussels) and Hughes were unearthed, living quietly and comfortably with the village priest and his old housekeeper. The priest was a dear old man with sound and philosophical ideas on the marché noir, *which he insisted should in many of its 'beneficial' activities merely be labelled 'le* marché parallel'. *He possessed some excellent brandy, and his Household Cavalry guests drank, between Christmas services, to the successful outcome of the Battle of the Bulge. I seem to recall that one session was interrupted by a ring on the doorbell and a parishioner came in with a 'marché parallel' boiling fowl, which the old priest promptly secreted under his cassock with a gentle smile.*

In their turn the echelons repaid calls, bringing adequate allocations of cigarettes, gin and whisky and other N.A.A.F.I. supplies collected by Captain Firth and his staff. R.Q.M.S. Goody and the storeman, Corporal Wincombe, could always be relied upon to get that something extra from the supply point, and this time they had excelled themselves.

There was champagne, and the men soon found out how to obtain sacks of freshly baked American white bread. We bought bottles of sickly sweet beer which tasted like bad Guinness and treacle, and discovered some 'Burgundy' in Huy, purchased at an outrageous price and fortified with chips of sandalwood and colouring matter. We exchanged bully beef for eggs and cigarettes for cheese, and a Belgian barber in Ardenne offered free haircuts and shampoos to the men. One Household Cavalryman, a road-mender in civilian life, came back in some confusion,

---

[180] *The Household Cavalry at War: Second Household Cavalry Regiment* by Roden Orde, published by Gale & Polden, Aldershot in 1953, reproduced by kind permission of Mrs Antonia Lloyd.

reeking of scent and having had his eyebrows plucked. With a nice feeling for foreign habits, he explained: 'I didn't dare stop the barber because I felt that this might be a Belgian custom at Christmas time.'

1944

Lieutenant Mary Louise Carpenter, US Army Nursing Corps, was with 13th Field Hospital and wrote to her family in Winchester, Massachusetts on 29 December:[181]

We arrived in time to get somewhat settled before supper, Brownie and I in a small room on the second floor of an isolation ward of a large Catholic hospital . . . the next morning some machine-gun fire was going on, about four blocks away, and one of our officers said he didn't know what the firing was about but that it was small arms, and it would be wise if we packed our musette bags (lightly) to make a quick get-away . . .

At breakfast the next morning there was an unexpressed feeling of triumph that we hadn't been moved and that a crisis had been weathered . . . we expected to spend Christmas peacefully in our isolation wards, and soon after breakfast the smell of roasting turkey pervaded the building. Very soon after came orders, pack up and move. By 01.30 we nurses were again packed up into ambulances with only our small luggage this time (our bedrolls, etc, were all in another vehicle) for a ride through wintry, war-pocked countryside, and through one large city of death where the houses are all empty shells.

We arrived at our destination in time to settle in a flimsy looking but not uncomfortable barracks before going to our turkey dinner at our mess hall. In the evening we opened little presents we had placed for each other under a small tree we had brought and decorated with ornaments taken no doubt from ruined German houses — lovely, original things like white-stemmed, sparkly, red-topped mushrooms and a pretty, gold-robed doll angel. Then the officers came in and we drank gin and grapefruit juice and ate Shrafft's nuts, and fruitcake until it really was Christmas. Christmas Day itself was sparkling clear. Such was the war at the time of the German breakthrough as I saw it.

[181] *Voices from the Battle of the Bulge* by Nigel de Lee, published by David & Charles in 2004.

1944

Rosemary Landheldt worked for the American Red Cross at Southampton docks. In her diary she wrote:[182]

The day before Christmas eve we started work at 04.00 to feed several shiploads of troops. Just as we were finally finished, the boys were suddenly offloaded, and I was informed the ships were to reload that night with infantry replacements. A high-security operation and a real rush job because of the German drive in the Bulge. I already had made crew assignments for Christmas week and knew several of us hoped to grab a few free hours to be with friends after finishing work. But when I asked for volunteers (sure to be six extra hours — at least — in the middle of the night on a bone-chilling cold, damp, and foggy docks), all I got was the usual 'Okay, coach, which piers and how many?' It's no wonder I love my crew. The division being rushed over was the 66th. On December 23rd, they were yanked out of camp so fast — without any notice — they still wore 66th Black Panther Division patches on their uniforms. Usually all division insignia is removed if it's a high security operation. The cooks had to leave stuffed turkeys and Christmas dinner preparations behind. They'd all had Christmas parties planned and suddenly they were eating K rations and headed for a channel crossing. Always especially tough in winter. They dragged into the dock area exhausted and it was easy to see they were not in a happy frame of mind. They began arriving early evening and our crews were there to serve units before the Port started loading the two troopships waiting at Pier 38: the British-controlled Léopoldville, a huge Belgian passenger liner, and the SS Cheshire. It was so cold in the dock sheds some of the guys lit bonfires to try and keep warm during the long wait . . . The men seemed so young. Many carried Christmas-wrapped boxes or goodies that wouldn't fit into their packs and they told us they were determined to celebrate Christmas wherever they happened to be. I used the Joker, the wonderful Canadian truck Tom gave us, to check supplies and shuttle more coffee and doughnuts where needed. By the time I drove into Pier 38 the troops crowded into that huge cavernous shell were in full-voiced rendition of 'White Christmas', the reverberating sound of thousands of voices seeming

---

[182] *Voices from the Battle of the Bulge* by Nigel de Lee, published by David & Charles in 2004.

to swell the shed in a mighty plea. I broke out all over in goosebumps. Eloise and Kari were in charge of our main Clubmobile and I noticed their eyes misted over too. For hours we served the men, and sang and talked and laughed with them. We did, as usual, a lot of listening and admiring pictures in wallets. We lingered past midnight to stand by the gangplank and wish the last units well and cheer them off as they finally boarded. It was so dark you couldn't see much, but every now and then a GI leaned over to kiss one of us on the cheek or give an awkward one-handed pat on the shoulder.

The following evening, when just five miles off Cherbourg, the *Léopoldville* was torpedoed and sunk by U-486, with the loss of almost 800 lives.

1944

When the Battle of the Bulge was finally over, a Belgian schoolteacher returned to his ruined classroom to find a message written on the blackboard:[183]

May the world never again live through such a Christmas night. Nothing is more horrible than meeting one's fate, far from mother, wife and children. Is it worthy of man's destiny to bereave a mother of her son, a wife of her husband, or children of their father? Life was bequeathed us in order that we might love and be considerate to one another. From the ruins, out of blood and death shall come forth a brotherly world.

(signed) *A German officer*

---

[183] *A Desperate Gamble* by Heike Hasenauer.

1944

In October 1939 Peter Robert Russell White enrolled as a student at the Royal Academy of Arts. In May 1942 he enlisted in the Royal Artillery, was commissioned a year later and transferred to the infantry in April 1944 to command 10 Platoon, B Company, 4th Battalion, King's Own Scottish Borderers. After clearing the island of Walcheren as part of Operation *Infatuate* in early November, the Battalion spent Christmas entrenched opposite their German foes in Tripsrath Woods on the Dutch/German border:[184]

On these clear frosty nights of silent, tense waiting D Company had night after night become familiar with the sound of a horse clip-clopping over the frozen roads behind the enemy lines. It became evident that its occupation was in bringing up rations and supplies at always, German fashion, the exact same time. This horse came to be known as 'Pinkie' by the Jocks. The meticulous exactness of the German routine put a great strain on the horse-loving OC of D Company.[185] Finally, the claims of war could be set aside no longer and with reluctance poor old Pinkie and his German masters for the last time exactly on schedule coincided with a prearranged shattering of the silence with a hail of high explosive. We never knew of the exact result as far as the ration party was concerned, but sadly Pinkie's leisurely walk never again sounded over the frozen night landscape.

I was personally rather sorry to hear that a similar fate had overcome a lusty choir of 'Stille Nacht' accompanied by an harmonium, which melodious and haunting sound had floated from the German lines on Christmas Eve. However, the Germans were not to be put off their carol singing so easily. Despite the efforts of the forward observation officer of the artillery and the sustained efforts of the guns, singing continued at intervals with such persistence that it was concluded that there must have been quite a heavy consumption of

[184] *With the Jocks*, published by Sutton Publishing Ltd in 2001: reprinted by kind permission of the publishers.
[185] Captain Charles Marrow, a first cousin of my mother.

schnapps as well as the harmonium as the accompaniment!

The CO and the Padre had succeeded, I heard, in visiting all the companies on Christmas Day, the Padre to hold a service and 'Chris', as he was known by all, to toast victory with the rum ration. Thus it was hoped all needs of 'the spirit' were met.

After the war Peter White returned to the Royal Academy and graduated in 1951. Finding it difficult to settle down, he travelled extensively – by motorcycle or by car and caravan – for the next fifteen years before marrying in 1972 and becoming a successful portrait painter. He died at Aldeburgh on 7 November 1985, at the age of sixty-four. His diary was only discovered after his death.

1944

On 19 August 1942, at a dance in the Officers' Club at Shillong, an Indian hill station, eighteen year-old Betty Stork met 'a rude but very attractive officer'. Two days later Magnus Gray, 7th Cameronians, wrote to her: 'A tall and beautiful wench has come across my path so quickly, so purely, so strongly that I know I want, and will want, to be with you more and more.' After following one another across a war-torn world, they were married at Comrie in Perthshire on 20 May 1944. After just weeks together, Major Magnus Gray went with his battalion to North-West Europe. On Boxing Day he wrote to Betty: [186]

Your wonderful letter of 20.12.44 arrived exactly on Christmas Day, yesterday and again Melville manfully came to me with it.[187] *I think it was an excuse too to give me his own personal greetings. Thank you for writing . . . I am sure you are not telling me of all your feelings in case it makes me anxious so instead you tell me what you are* <u>doing</u>; *perhaps at this moment it is best this way. You leave me thinking that you walk a lonely path but that you are in full command of the situation, and that you have hope, perhaps not in the immediate future, but for things to come. That is some comfort for me . . .*

This was roughly the Christmas programme. Reveille 0800, Breakfast 0900. At 1000 there was the Church parade with the C.S.M. manfully playing on an old piano. I sat next to the C.O. and enjoyed singing the carols more than ever. After the service two other junior officers and I dashed off to the chaps left outside in the trenches and we did a quick recce to see that all was well. I was to spend the day with my own Company and while I was away on the recce the rest of my Company officers and sergeants prepared the Christmas dinner for our men. Each man had a can of beer, a bag of sweets, a packet of cigarettes, two apples and an orange. Also they had an

[186] The papers of Mrs M. Gray in the Imperial War Museum Documents Collection: by kind permission of Mrs Betty Donaldson. In the autobiographical *My Man* by Marjorie Gray, the author refers to herself as Emmaline, and to her future husband as Peter White.
[187] Adrian Melville, his batman.

enormous plate of pork and tinned turkey followed by Christmas pudding and fruit salad. The officers and N.C.O.s waited at table. We had also managed to gather quite a bit of drink. I think our cellar consisted of 14 bottles of whisky, 7 of brandy, 10 champagne and 4 gin. As there were 115 of us you can imagine that it all went in one afternoon and evening. Fortunately no-one put up any blacks. After this huge meal which we only served but did not eat the officers and sergeants sat down to one for themselves later on in the evening. This was a great success and it ended up in a sing-song, everyone by now being in very good form. When all this was over the C.S.M. and I went round all the individual billets and demanded a song. Many and varied were the songs sung and the lads were in splendid form, and most of them said that it was the best Christmas that they had had in the Army, but I'm such an old stager that I realise that all the troops say that every Christmas. (Damn — while I am writing a German plane has just flown over and machine-gunned part of the town. There are quite a large number of single German aircraft about these days, but our A.A., however, is so effective that we manage to shoot many of them down.) When I was due to turn in Melville insisted in accompanying me all the way to the cellar, and sat me on my bed to take off my boots. I think he must have thought I was tiddly, but I thought I was well in control of myself. The best part of the whole day was when I proposed the toast 'Wives and Sweethearts' and I drank to you.

Today we had an easy day, but I went to the concert produced by Bill Foster. It was rather disappointing, for a lot of effort had been put into it, but the hall was not full, and it needed a crowd of people to respond to the bawdy jokes. At the end one youngster stood still and alone and sang 'Silent Night'. I don't think I have ever heard it sung better, and a tell-tale lump came in my throat and I could not help wishing that you were listening to it too.

So that is how we spent our Christmas at the Front. It is strange to have to switch from camaraderie to war so quickly. It is also difficult to realise that the enemy in their dug-outs not far away are mostly just lads of the same calibre as the ones I look after, and that I am trained as a soldier to shoot at these young lads as an enemy. I am also trained to defend my country and the principles that we have gone to war to protect, and if the enemy threaten those principles and my country then I have to shoot first, and prove that I am an efficient professional. To consider the enemy as a group of young lads following orders from their superior officers is a thought that has to be pushed to the back of the mind without further reasoning.

Major Magnus Gray was shot by a sniper in Obspringen, Germany on 22 January 1945. Adrian Melville wrote to his widow: 'We managed to get him to the Field Dressing Centre where he was terribly cheerful, as he always was. I was with him most of the evening, and all the time he was talking to the other casualties and took no notice of himself. He said his wounds were small and not as bad as the others. I left him that night waiting for medical attention to take off the bandages that we had put on. When I went the next morning to see how he was I found he had died. I am told he died through loss of blood, and I am told that, if he had more attention paid to himself and not made light of his wounds telling the staff to look after the others first, he would have been saved.'

1944

From Springwood, his home on the Hudson River in the Hyde Park area of New York City, US President Franklin D. Roosevelt broadcast to the nation:

It is not easy to say 'Merry Christmas' to you, my fellow Americans, in this time of destructive war. Nor can I say 'Merry Christmas' lightly tonight to our armed forces at their battle stations all over the world — or to our Allies who fight by their side. Here, at home, we will celebrate this Christmas Day in our traditional American way — because of its deep spiritual meaning to us; because the teachings of Christ are fundamental in our lives; and because we want our youngest generation to grow up knowing the significance of this tradition and the story of the coming of the immortal Prince of Peace and Good-Will. But, in perhaps every home in the United States, sad and anxious thoughts will be continually with the millions of our loved ones who are suffering hardships and misery, and who are risking their very lives to preserve for us and mankind the fruits of His teachings and the foundations of civilization itself.

The Christmas spirit lives tonight in the bitter cold of the front lines in Europe and in the heat of the jungles and swamps of Burma and the Pacific islands. Even the roar of our bombers and fighters in the air and the guns of our ships at sea will not drown out the messages of Christmas which come to the hearts of our fighting men. The thoughts of those men tonight will turn to us here at home around our Christmas trees, surrounded by our children and grandchildren and their Christmas stockings and gifts — just as our own thoughts go out to them, tonight and every night, in their distant places. We all know how anxious they are to be home with us, and they know how anxious we are to have them — and how determined every one of us is to make their day of home-coming as early as possible. And — above all — they know the determination of all right thinking people and nations, that Christmases such as those that we have known in these years of world tragedy shall not come again to beset the souls of the children of God.

This generation has passed through many recent years of deep darkness, watching the spread of the poison of Hitlerism and fascism in Europe — the growth of imperialism and militarism in Japan — and the final clash of war all over the world. Then came the dark days of the fall of

France, and the ruthless bombing of England, and the desperate battle of the Atlantic, and of Pearl Harbor and Corregidor and Singapore. Since then the prayers of good men and women and children the world over have been answered. The tide of battle has turned, slowly but inexorably, against those who sought to destroy civilization. And so, on this Christmas Day, we cannot yet say when our victory will come. Our enemies still fight fanatically. They still have reserves of men and military power. But, they themselves know that they and their evil works are doomed. We may hasten the day of their doom if we here at home continue to do our full share. And we pray that day may come soon. We pray that until then, God will protect our gallant men and women in the uniforms of the United Nations — that He will receive into His infinite grace those who make their supreme sacrifice in the cause of righteousness, in the cause of love of Him and His teachings. We pray that with victory will come a new day of peace on earth in which all the nations of the earth will join together for all time. That is the spirit of Christmas, the holy day. May that spirit live and grow throughout the world in all the years to come.

Franklin D. Roosevelt, thirty-second President of the United States, died on 12 April 1945 at Warm Springs, Georgia.

1944

Christabel Burton, a niece of the newspaper barons, Lord Northcliffe, Viscount Rothermere and Lord Harmsworth, went to Hamburg in 1932 to train as a singer under Alma Schadow.[188] She married Peter Bielenberg, a trainee lawyer, moved to Berlin and they had three sons. While her husband worked for the German war machine, Christabel took her sons to the Black Forest to escape the bombing. Following the 20 July 1944 plot against Hitler, Peter Bielenberg was arrested and held at Ravensbrück, where Christabel was on her way to visit him: [189]

It was late afternoon and everyone seemed to be hurrying somewhere. Of course, it was Christmas Eve. We had celebrated a day early in Rohrbach — a long time ago yesterday. A little wooden toy carved by our Pole Josef for Christopher, and for Nick and John two precious penknives sent by Outram through the Swedish Embassy, and saved up since last March. A tree too, brought down from the woods by Nick, and decorated with the silver foil which strewed the fields after the Allied bombers had droned over us, bound for Munich or Augsburg. We were told it was meant to disturb radio communications. Maybe it did that too, but it certainly came in useful at Christmas. It was not yet time for the blackout, and through the gaily lighted windows I could hear the music and watch the busy Christmas preparations. I amused myself trying to imagine what kind of people lived in the houses, by looking at their Christmas trees . . . Beside each tree the lighted crib. True, I was in Catholic Germany, but even so it was reassuring that Hitler had seemingly not yet succeeded in banishing that symbol from so many homes. But now, as I looked closer, even the trees had a more uniform look. Odd length candles, left-overs from other years. No sweets; the lametta, except for where the Allied silver foil had come to the rescue, ragged and tarnished; the presents not very numerous and not much to write home about either.

[188] The teacher of the well-known operatic sopranos and Lieder singers, Elisabeth Schumann and Lotte Lehmann.
[189] *The Past is Myself*, published by Chatto & Windus in 1968: reprinted by kind permission of The Random House Group Ltd.

It was rather a lonely business, however, just being outside of it all, and as the shutters closed one by one I began to feel a bit sorry for myself. I made my way back to the station waiting room. A scraggy-looking Christmas tree had been rigged up in the corner and the waitress, who was standing behind an empty counter, surrounded by empty glass shelves, had turned on the wireless which was playing slow sentimental Christmas music, O Tannebaum — Süsser die Glocken nie klingen — Stille Nacht. A large, highly-coloured oil painting of Hitler — the work, no doubt, of some local Velasquez — hung on the wall beside the wireless and stared down morosely at the coffee urn.

After the war the Bielenbergs bought a farm at Munny in County Carlow, 50 miles south of Dublin. Christabel Bielenberg died on 2 November 2003.

1944

With her mother, her sister Sophie and her 'Auntie' Maria Bulat, Janina Bauman was deported from the Warsaw Ghetto in the summer of 1944: they were taken in by the Pietrzyks, a Christian family from the village of Zielonki, near Kracòw. Many years later she wrote:[190]

We felt very uneasy about the approaching festivities, fearing we might do something wrong and show our ignorance of Christian traditions. To make it worse, two ladies from Warsaw who had befriended Auntie Maria in the queue for free meals, insisted on spending Christmas Eve with her, but claimed that the place they lived in was not good enough for the occasion. Auntie Maria could hardly say no, which meant they would come, meet the rest of us and be able to watch us closely for hours. We really dreaded it. On the morning of the crucial day we dressed our fragrant tree, and, very pleased with ourselves since it looked gorgeous, called Mrs Pietrzyk in to let her see and marvel at it. The old woman scanned the tree, nodding with approval, then stepped back and glanced at the top with special attention. Her expression changed, her jaw dropped, she clearly did not like what she saw. Taken aback, I followed her gaze to the top of the tree and shuddered: in full daylight against the background of the whitewashed wall stood a six-pointed blue star of David, the emblem of the Jews. Mrs Pietrzyk said nothing and left, but after a while she came back with a golden cardboard angel of impressive size. 'This would look better, if you ask me,' she said flatly. We didn't quite know what she really meant.

Christmas Eve, which we had dreaded so much, turned out rather well. The two Warsaw women arrived in festive mood and seemed very friendly. One of them, a dressmaker, had lost her husband in the war, the other, a chiropodist, was a spinster. We had an almost traditional supper, since Mrs Pietrzyk presented us with borsch and noodles with poppy seed, and the ladies also brought some food to share. Before we began, all the Pietrzyk family came in for a while to break the wafers with us. Then we sang carols and really enjoyed ourselves: despite our early misgivings everything worked out fine. As we parted from our visitors, the dressmaker warmly embraced

---

[190] *Winter in the Morning – A Young Girl's Life in the Warsaw Ghetto and Beyond 1939–45*, published by Virago in 1986.

Mother and said, '*Hope for the best, my dear. You've endured the worst, God will help you till the end.*' '*It won't be long now,*' chimed in the chiropodist. They had both guessed our secret.

In May 1945 Janina Bauman retrieved 'all my copybooks and loose sheets covered with my untidy handwriting, hidden safely in a hole in the floor, under a few bricks'.

1944

Having been captured during the desperate fighting for Lebisey Wood, near Caen, Normandy in June 1944, Captain Alastair Bannerman, Royal Warwickshire Regiment, a professional actor in civilian life, was now confined in Oflag 79 near Braunschweig (Brunswick), from where he wrote to his wife, Elisabeth:[191]

Xmas morning and the sun is shining and the frost lies in patterns across the window. God bless you, my family, my heart is with you. I went to a Carol Service at 4.30 yesterday and thought of you and Andrew and Richard having a tree and presents and I was very close. O come let us adore Him *I sang as if we were round your piano. In the evening we had a band show until 11.30 and then I went to Midnight Communion in the cellar that is our chapel. What a strange life it all is here. Barbed wire and machine guns keep us in, but we make quite a lot of our confined life. A bit like university with a touch of Broadmoor! This morning I opened my stocking (a sock!) with chocolate and snaps from you, which amazingly arrived on the eve. So lovely to glimpse you again, and so Xmassy to look at them by the light of dawn. I've saved enough food to be really full today, anyhow, with fried bread and potatoes, marmalade and coffee for breakfast. (Red X parcels still trickle through, but I guess not much longer.)*

I've been asked to read the lesson at 11.00 Matins, great honour! For lunch, pea soup and choc. Tea, I've made a cake (and/or pudding) from biscuits and prunes, and iced it with milk powder. Also painted a card symbolising our love, joining prison and Sandford Cottage across the seas and distance, pinned up over my top bunk. German stew for supper – ugh! We're doing a Round the Empire Xmas *show tonight in our underground cabaret* Xmas Pie *and I am appearing in a beard as the old spirit of 1944 saying good-bye to this year! Some prisoners are spending their 5th Xmas 'in the bag', a bit grim and hardly merry. But the news is good and they are very courageous and patient. It is very cold, no hot water, but have enough clothes. But do send pyjamas, towel,*

---

[191] *As With Your Shadow* by Alastair and Elisabeth Bannerman, published by Creeds, Bridport: reprinted by kind permission of Alastair Bannerman.

choc and toothbrush and paste if you can! Your love and image is always my strength, and I thank God for many mercies. I love you.

Determined that some good should result from their captivity, the prisoners of war in Oflag 79 pledged money for 'a club in which every officer would have an interest and which would grow into a living denial of the futility of those war years'. The results – Brunswick Boys' Club in Fulham and Brunswick Youth Club in Bootle – are still flourishing.

1944

In 1934 Agnes Newton married Harry George Keith, Conservator of Forests and Director of Agriculture in British North Borneo, and went to live at Sandakan, one of just seventy-five Europeans in the capital of British North Borneo. Agnes Keith wrote *Land Below The Wind*, published in November 1939 and based on her experiences in the colony. After the Japanese invaded British North Borneo on 19 January 1942, Agnes Keith and her twenty-one month-old son George were soon interned, for the first year on Berhala Island and subsequently at Kuching, the capital of neighbouring Sarawak. Her book had been translated into Japanese and was widely read by her captors. Of her third Christmas in captivity with George she wrote:[192]

In the afternoon we had the Christmas tree. It had been sent from the men's camp with all the decorations on it, made by the civilian men and the British soldiers, and arranged for by George Colley, the American from Manila. The tree was pleasant, a small Dacrydium *with bending boughs. Flowers and tiny scraps of coloured cloth or string or paper were used to make it bright. There was a present on it for every child from the sender, and a few children had additional gifts. The smaller gifts were hung on the tree, and the heavy ones placed under. It was like every Christmas tree, the shrine of great promise. A Christmas angel in spangles with limbs of seduction and face of enticing dissipation teetered drunkenly on top, created by a British Tommy, in likeness of a prisoner's dream.*

Long before the presents were distributed the boys had spotted the best ones. These were the two wooden motor trucks, a train, and a large and splendid ship carved of rubberwood. These were outstanding and stupendous, they were manly and pretentious. All over the tree were hung various coloured stuffed animals and dolls which represented Mamma's garments and undergarments of

[192] From *Three Came Home: A mother's ordeal in a Japanese prison camp* by Agnes Keith, published by Eland Books in 2002 [1948]: reproduced by permission of Eland Books.

the past — most ingenious, considering — considering! The materials for these had been sent to the men to work with; and there were giraffes, tigers, elephants, zebras, spotted ponies, dogs, cats, bunnies, golliwogs — whimsical, fanciful, phony. We thought they were wonderful, considering . . . considering . . . But who wants to consider?

After the war Harry, Agnes and George went back to Sandakan, where they stayed until 1952. Agnes wrote a third book about Borneo, this time entitled *White Man Returns*. After living in the Philippines and Libya, she and Harry retired to Victoria, British Columbia, where she died in the late 1990s.

1944

Sister Enid Palmer, the daughter of a Conservator of Forests and his wife, a doctor, who had retired to Kalaw in the southern Shan States of Burma, trained in Rangoon and joined the Burma Hospital Nursing Corps, later the Burma Military Nursing Service. She was stationed at No. 41 Indian General Hospital (Combined), which cared for Indian, African and British troops, on the plains of Imphal in Manipur State, India. On 29 December she wrote to her parents, who had been hurriedly evacuated from Burma in March 1942 and were living at Nakuru in Kenya:[193]

My Dear Mum & Dad,

I'm afraid I have not written to you for some time — life has been one mad rush lately what with Christmas etc. Thank you ever so much for the lovely parcels you sent through the K.W.C. — they were full of nice things & I love the jersey you have knitted me — it is just what I have been wanting for a long while.

The mat brightens up the tent & is very nice indeed. I have had a very happy Christmas indeed. I have enjoyed every minute of it. It has been spent mostly with the patients, trying to entertain them, & I think they have all had a very happy time. On the 21st we had our party, I think I told you all about it in my last letter. On Christmas Eve, Scottie, Geoff, Coral, one other Sister & I went over to the old site where two British patients had been left for Christmas & we all set up a Christmas tree for them & the other boys went over & decorated the ward for them. They were too ill to be moved over here for Xmas.

On the way home, we went to the Airstrip & saw the Father Christmas which was going to be dropped to forward troops on Christmas Day. He was made of red cloth & stuffed with grain & had a lovely beard. I should love to have seen him floating down by parachute.

[193] The papers of Miss E. D. C. Palmer in the Imperial War Museum Documents Collection: by kind permission of Mrs Enid Grant.

On Christmas Day Father Christmas came round the hospital on an elephant. He went from ward to ward & gave each patient a present. The same afternoon, was their Christmas dinner, then at 3 o'clock an excellent concert got up by the Sisters, orderlies & patients. On the 26th we had a tea party in our mess to which all the patients & M.O.'s & orderlies came. There was a Christmas tree & Father Christmas gave the presents away. After which we sat round the fire singing.

I hope you have had a very happy Christmas too. Thanks again ever so much. Write soon.

Lots of love & kisses from

xx *Enid* xx

Enid Palmer spent VJ Day in Rangoon, went to live in Kenya after the war and later married Alastair Grant, who worked for MI6.

1944

Flying Officer Harold Gardner was serving with Section 16, RAF Ceylon. On 29 December he wrote to his sister Mabel, who was living at 372 Larks Hall Road, Chingford:[194]

Thank you for your Christmas Airgraph & for your letter (no. 30) of 5th November enclosing copy of Trinity Magazine. Regarding the latter I'm sorry you went to the expense of sending it by air mail; it is hardly quicker than sea mail — Edna & I found that out long ago & seldom make use of the service. You see this one took seven weeks! Well, my last Christmas overseas, and my best, is over. Let me tell you about it. It actually started for me several days before Christmas for I always think that the preparation is more pleasurable than the event itself. We — the Rover Crew — thought we'd hold our own party on Christmas night. Our fellows are all decent chaps who object to the horseplay & drunkenness that are always the outstanding feature of Christmas at any camp, so we decided to get away from it. I was in charge of 'effects' — but, unfortunately, the town is out of bounds owing to an outbreak of smallpox, so that I could not purchase anything, & we had to improvise. It saved money, & we had the fun of making things. We made paper chains by cutting up coloured covers of magazines & by painting scrap paper; we decorated the Radjan walls with fronds of palm leaves; we made memento cards for autographs; &, above all, we hewed down a cactus bush which we used as a Christmas tree, & it was just perfect with bonbons (which we were fortunate to obtain), & small gifts of cigarettes, razor blades, &c. &c. which we purchased from our N.A.A.F.I. In fact I really think the cactus is better than a spruce fir — it carries the weight better — but I guarantee it's the first time in history that a cactus has been used for this purpose! We had the whole photographed (indoors) — I hope the result will be good.

On Christmas evening, then, after a reasonably good dinner in the Mess, 26 of us adjourned to the Hut, & we stayed there until 2 a.m.! We played games & sang songs & carols — &, of

---

[194] The papers of Flying Officer H. E. Gardner in the Imperial War Museum Documents Collection: every effort has been made to trace copyright holders and the author and the Imperial War Museum would be grateful for any information which might help to trace those whose identities or addresses are not currently known.

course, smoked & drank 'pop', & ate tinned fruit, & biscuits, & peanuts! It was <u>very</u> successful indeed — & will, I'm sure, strengthen the Crew for the future, apart from being a Happy Christmas. I helped to serve the airmen with their Christmas dinner in traditional Service style. On Sunday evening we had a Carol Service — the first service in our Camp Church. The Church is yet another Radjan but adapted for the purpose, & the furnishings are the work of the men. It holds about 100, & was full! There were other services, & sports events, & cinema shows & concerts on the camp — but other duties or other preferences didn't allow me, of course, to be at them all. Anyhow it was a very good Christmas, & I trust it was for you also.

1944

Mary Hilbert spent Christmas with her family in Seattle:[195]

We dreaded Christmas that year. It was 1944, and the war would never be over for our family. The telegram had arrived in August. Bob's few personal possessions, the flag from his coffin, the plat of his burial site in the Philippines, a Distinguished Flying Cross had arrived one by one, adding to our agonising grief. Born on a midwestern prairie, my brother rode horseback to school but wanted to fly an airplane from the day he first saw one. By the time he was twenty-one, we were living in Seattle. When World War II broke out, Bob headed for the nearest recruitment office . . . When he was named Hot Pilot of primary training school in Pasco, Wash., and later involuntarily joined the 'Caterpillar Club' (engine failure causing the bailout) at St. Mary's, California, we shook our heads and worried. Mother prayed. Bob was born fearless, and she knew it. Before graduating, he applied for a transfer to the Marine Air Corps at Pensacola, Fla. He trained in torpedo bombers before being sent overseas. They said Bob died under enemy fire over New Guinea in the plane he so desperately wanted to fly. Mother's faith sustained her, but my father aged before our eyes. He would listen politely when the minister came to call, but we knew Daddy was bitter. He dragged himself to work every day but lost interest in everything else, including his beloved Masonic Club. He'd wanted a Masonic ring real bad, and at Mother's insistence, he'd started saving for the ring, but that, too, ceased. I dreaded the approach of Christmas. Bob had loved Christmas. His surprises were legendary: a doll house made at school, a puppy hidden in a mysterious place for our little brother, an expensive dress for Mother bought with the very first money he ever earned. Everything had to be a surprise. What would Christmas be without Bob? Not much. Aunts, uncles and Grandmother were coming, so we went through the motions as much for memory as anything, but our hearts weren't in it. On 23 December, another official-looking package arrived. My father watched stone-faced as Mother unpacked Bob's dress blues. Silence hung heavy. As she refolded the uniform to put it away, a mother's practicality surfaced, and she went through the pockets almost by rote. In a small inside jacket pocket was a

---

[195] *Dead Son's Special Gift of Healing Love Helps Save Christmas* by Mary Hilbert, *Houston Chronicle*, 20 December 1998: reprinted by kind permission of Mary Hilbert.

neatly folded $50 bill with a tiny note in Bob's familiar handwriting: 'For Dad's Masonic Ring.' If I live to be one hundred, I will never forget the look on my father's face. Some kind of transformation took place — a touch of wonder, a hint of joy, a quiet serenity that was glorious to behold. Oh, the healing power of love! He stood transfixed, staring at the note and the trimly folded bill in his hand for what seemed an eternity, then walked to Bob's picture hanging prominently on the wall and solemnly saluted. 'Merry Christmas, son,' he murmured and turned to welcome Christmas.

1945

On Christmas Eve Walter L. Cronkite, later to become a legend as the anchorman of *CBS News*, filed a story for *The Washington Times-Herald* on the funeral at Hamm Cemetery, Luxembourg, of General George S. Patton, who had died three days previously from injuries received in a motor accident:[196]

Gen George S. Patton joined the dead heroes of his 3d Army today beneath the thick, red clay of the Ardennes, where they had fought together just a year ago. Patton was buried the morning of this Christmas Eve in what he himself once had called 'damned poor tank country and damned bad weather'. But he was buried in a precision-like military ceremony touched by pomp and tendered by grief. Big generals and little soldiers were there, as were royalty and the commoners of this tiny country from which Patton drove the Germans in that crucial battle last Christmastide. But the focal figure, standing there under the dark sky against the background of green hills, was Patton's widow. A raw wind, whirling across the top of the blue on which the cemetery is located, ruffled Mrs. Patton's veil as she watched the ceremony at the grave, no different from the other 7,933 others topped by white crosses. Her eyes were red, but for the rest she was the same good soldier her husband had been.

In the final minute of the ceremony M/Sgt. William G. Meeks, the negro from Junction City, Kansas, who had served Patton faithfully as his orderly for eight years, presented the general's widow with the flag that had draped the coffin. There were tears in Meeks's eyes. His face was screwed up with strain. He bowed slowly, and handed the flag to Mrs. Patton. Then he saluted stiffly to her. For an instant their eyes met and held. Meeks turned away, a twelve-man firing squad raised its rifles and a three-round volley of salutes echoed into the Luxembourg hills. The bugler played the soft, sad notes of 'taps'.[197] The twenty-five-minute burial ceremony was over. It was 10.15 A.M. in Luxembourg . . .

[196] *The Washington Times-Herald*, 25 December 1945: reproduced by kind permission of Walter Cronkite, journalist, WWII correspondent, UP.

[197] *Taps* is a bugle call, standard at US military funerals since 1891, which was composed by Major-General Daniel Adams Butterfield, United States Army, in 1862.

Mrs. Patton took a last look at the casket while an aide placed a wreath of camellias on the top. The coffin was not lowered into the grave because of the wet weather. The general's widow returned to her limousine where, for ten minutes, she received the condolences of the visiting generals. Then she drove to the Luxembourg station to entrain for Paris. From there, reports said tonight, she took a plane from Orly Airfield for the United States. That was Mrs. Patton's Christmas Eve.

1950

Emory Leon 'Buddy' Roe of Salem, North Carolina, was born on 21 December 1931, enlisted in the US Army on 26 August 1949 and soon went to Korea with 70th Tank Battalion. On 19 August 1950 he wrote home, rather optimistically, from the 'Pusan Perimeter':[198]

I could see them moving out over the hills like flys [sic], all I had to do was cut loose, it was like shooting ducks on the pond, well I've got my share of them already, that's what I like about tanks, you sure get your share of them. Now don't think I'm getting hard hearted by killing so much because if you would see some of our boys after they get a hold of them you would do the same thing, the dirty rats. But don't worry they will never get a hold of me. I would have more pity on a snake than these damn Gooks.

The reality of the situation soon impressed itself on 'Buddy' Roe. On 27 November he wrote to his brother Harold from 'Land of Paridise [sic], Korea':

Boy Harold, I'm really hoping that something like this doesn't happen over there, while your still there. It's really a bloody mess. I've seen many, many GIs get hell blown out of them, so came pretty close to it myself.

As the United Nations forces retreated all the way back to the South Korean border, he wrote to 'Mom, Dad, all' on 23 December:

I'm telling you this roughing it is beginning to work on my bones. I wouldn't mind it so bad, if they would at least feed us, we get two meals a day, breakfast and supper, and then there's not enough to know you even ate, we sure are putting away the rice though. But plain rice just doesn't get it.

[198] Published by kind permission of Julian Heward.

You would be surprised at all the Gook words I've picked up, enough to get by on anyway. I can say them, but I couldn't write them. Oh yes, right now we're on the side of the Imjin river about twenty five miles from the 38th . . . Boy it was really hard to withdraw all the way back here, after fighting so hard to get where we were and don't let the papers fool you about a statigec [sic] withdraw either. The Chings were first beating hell out of us, the Bn our Plattoon [sic] was with had just got hell beat out of us, when I wrote that last letter, but old Dugout Doug (MacArthur) got us out of there.[199] But now we're wondering if he's going to get us out of here all together . . . I stole a couple of chickens and had fried chicken and a can of beer on my birthday, not bad . . . I sure hope Lenora, and Sharon and Wanda have a very happy Xmas this year, tell them I'm always thinking of them and am sending them a bucket of kisses and hugs for the holidays . . . Please don't worry about me, I've lasted this long, and have sure been through it so you can bet on it I'm going the rest of the way. So long again.

Exactly two months later 'Buddy' Roe was killed in action near Wonju, South Korea.

[199] Despite his popularity with the troops, General Douglas MacArthur was unceremoniously removed from his post by US President Harry S. Truman on 11 April 1951.

1950/51

In the summer of 1947 regular British Army recruit Henry O'Kane from County Derry was reluctantly drafted from the Depôt of the Royal Inniskilling Fusiliers in Omagh – with which regiment he was too young to serve in India – to the 1st Battalion, Royal Ulster Rifles, then based at Klagenfurt in Austria. On 5 November 1950 he arrived at Pusan, Korea in the SS *Empire Pride*: 'As each man stepped on to the soil of Korea he was handed an apple by a shy Korean schoolgirl, part of a group who stood in their school uniforms of white blouse and long black high-waisted skirts, and who, with a solemn bow, murmured "thank you sir" as we passed.' 29th British Independent Infantry Brigade spent Christmas in defensive positions in the valley of a dried-up river bed about six miles north of Seoul. It was known as Compo Canyon since 'Compo rations, British Army issue, arrived from the quartermaster's depot daily'. Henry O'Kane later wrote:[200]

In Compo Canyon we spent our first Christmas in Korea. It was celebrated in comfort and as is usual in an Irish Battalion with a good deal of conviviality. The QM, Capt Tom Smith, had succeeded in securing enough turkey to feed the Battalion extremely well. Christmas pudding, a double ration of rum, an issue of canned beer plus a good supply of Korean Sake completed the feast. All the Korean houseboys were grouped together to sing Ari-ang *and other Korean melodies. They also managed a bit of* Silent Night *and* White Christmas. *The Pipes and Drums gave a rendering of Irish tunes and the Korean hills echoed to the sounds of* Paddy Carey, The Wearing of the Green *and similar Irish patriotic tunes. A good time was had by all.*

Henry O'Kane was captured on the Imjin River in late April 1951 and

---

[200] *O'Kane's Korea*, privately printed in 1988: reprinted by kind permission of Henry O'Kane.

spent the following Christmas at Chong-Song POW Camp, North Korea:

Local concert parties were put on at Christmas in the town's cinema by each company. The place was frozen but everyone struggled to get a place at each of the seven company concerts. All the material had to be passed by the Chinese censors. Much of it they could not or would not understand. For 7 Company's concert I once gave the censor the words for When Irish Eyes are Smiling *but the censor threw it out, remarking that the eyes did not smile, the mouth did! If we put mouth in he would allow it, truly believing that there was some hidden meaning or joke against themselves.*

Henry O'Kane was given a medical discharge in 1954 and is now secretary of the Hatton and District branch of The Royal British Legion.

1951

Second Lieutenant Lindsey Garrett Smith, Royal Tank Regiment, extended his National Service by a year in order to serve with the Commonwealth Division in Korea. After arriving in MV *Georgic* in late 1951, he was attached to the 5th Royal Inniskilling Dragoon Guards. On 22 December he wrote home:[201]

We have been here now for three weeks and are well settled, very little is happening except for vehicles getting ditched and breaking down generally on the roads which are entirely made from the country by our own engineers and consist of packed sand and mud which goes liquid when it rains and is full of potholes at all times. I got the parcels from Fortnums *for which I am very greatful [sic] and also your letter which was very welcome indeed.[202] Christmas this year will be quite subdued I think, we get a lot of turkey in our ordinary rations, huge birds from America weighing anything up to twenty four pounds but Xmas pudding is rationed to 8 2lb puddings to 100 men, but they will get free beer & chocolate.*

On Christmas Day he sent another letter to his parents:

I expect you have all had the normal round of Christmas festivities or will have had by the time you get this letter, I believe in facts although, it is five minutes to five in the afternoon here, you will just be getting up on Christmas morning to go to early service. I must say we are not very cheerful here. Last night we had some Canadians who made a lot of noise up till about three in the morning. They were all very tight and had been attracted by the lights of my cookhouse where the turkeys were being roasted on our field oven which is made out of a 50 gallon oil drum and corrugated iron. The noise kept a Major in HQ Squadron who lives about 200 yards away awake

---

[201] The papers of Lieutenant L. G. G. Smith in the Imperial War Museum Documents Collection: by kind permission of Major Lindsey Smith.
[202] In a letter of 27 June 2007 Lindsey Smith wrote: 'The *Fortnum* hampers were in fact consumed by the officers of A Sqn not me, but I did not tell my parents!'

and both Dave and I who had slept through almost all of it except the last when I went out and quelled the riot were not very popular.[203] *We did our best for the men, took them tea and rum in bed in the morning and served out the dinner which was very good, though a bit cold as we have no dining room. It started to hail in the morning, then snow till lunch, and now it is pouring with rain, and we are all very damp. But the men are in good heart and have lots of sweets and nuts and beer in moderation so that's all right. I am going to Kure in Japan on about the 27th which does not please me, but I expect you will be glad to hear.*

PS We had a bit of a battle yesterday. I wasn't there but apparently one tank got stuck and everyone flapped quite unnecessarily, not much on today though there was a lot of shelling on both sides last night. The doctor shot a deer, which looks like a dog and had big front teeth and no horns but tastes quite good. We had a Carol service this morning.

After returning to 6th Royal Tank Regiment in Germany, Lindsey Smith accepted the offer of a regular commission, learned to fly helicopters, and was seconded to the newly-formed Army Air Corps in 1957. He later saw service in Malaya and Borneo and, after retirement, was Curator of the Museum of Army Flying at Middle Wallop, Hampshire.

[203] In the letter quoted above, Lindsey Smith wrote that 'OC HQ Sqn was not amused and I was put under open arrest all Christmas day!'

1952

Captain Anthony Farrar-Hockley was Adjutant of the 1st Battalion, The Gloucestershire Regiment during the Imjin River battle on 22–25 April 1951 and was taken prisoner when Battalion Headquarters was overrun. While a prisoner of war he made no less than six attempts to escape, on one occasion managing to reach the coast before being recaptured. Later he was held in a camp at Pyoktong on the Yalu River and wrote of his last Christmas in captivity:[204]

Christmas Day 1952 was a memorable day — particularly the evening. An inter-denominational carol service was held about seven o'clock in a Library gaily decorated with paintings, streamers, and pine branches, the work of Guy, Recce, and the Sergeants-Major, led by Sergeant-Major Baker of our Support Company. Our thoughts were very naturally all of home and we were not in the best mood to receive an address from Ding, the Camp Commander, which Chang was to read to us at nine o'clock.

Chang sensed our mood. He knew that we should not be receptive to his good wishes after what he had to read out, so he extended them beforehand. It was principally an American audience, and Chang spoke with an American accent. 'Say, I've got a Christmas message from Commander Ding for all of you, and in a few minutes, I'm going to read it out. But before I do, I want to say "Happy Christmas" everyone. I hope that next year you'll all be back home with your families. Now here is the message from the Camp Commander.'

He began to read from a page of typescript in his hand, and his appreciations of our reactions had been accurate. It was in the worst possible taste; for, after starting mildly, Ding had been unable to restrain his fanaticism for the Communist cause. He quoted — or rather, misquoted — the Scriptures, particularly the teachings of Christ. We heard the beloved Christmas words, for instance, rendered as follows: 'Peace on earth to men of good will'; and the only men of good will, it seemed, were those who followed the policies of the Comintern group of governments. As Chang

---

[204] *The Edge of the Sword*, published by Frederick Muller in 1954: reprinted by kind permission of Sutton Publishing Ltd.

read on, the silence seemed to intensify. When he had finished, no one spoke; but I have neither felt nor seen before such profound disgust expressed silently by a body of men.

'That's all,' said Chang. He was not sorry for what had been said; only sorry that he had been the one who had had to say it, and so lose popularity.

General Sir Anthony Farrar-Hockley's experiences of communism may have stood him in good stead during his term as Commander-in-Chief, Allied Forces Northern Europe at the height of the 'Cold War'. He died on 11 March 2006.

1967

Sergeant John B. Jones spent Christmas at Dau Tieng, a strategic outpost in War Zone C, north-west of Saigon:[205]

There's no easy way around it . . . it's hell being away from home and your family at Christmas, especially during wartime. Everything is so iffy . . . so uncertain. You miss your folks like crazy, and your absence around the Christmas tree back home on Christmas morning is magnified by a factor of ten because of where you are and is almost more than the homefolks can handle . . .

Soon everybody was packed into the truck and/or hangin' on the sideboards; and, not wanting to waste time backing up to get a good aim at the gate, Sarge just drove the damn thing through the barbed fence (much to the painful dismay of the boys hanging precariously on the sideboards).

We had just enough time to sing another repetition of the chorus to Jingle Bells *(Jingle bells, jingle bells, jingle all the way . . . hm hm hm hm hm hm hm hm hm hm hm . . .) before pulling up in front of our designated goal. The priest, and other chaplains, had decorated the rough chapel and even had Christmas lights strung up across the front. Damn, but that was a pretty sight.*

We very unceremoniously unassed the truck and, laughing at the daring of our misdeed, entered the sacred house. We were still grab-assing and drinking when we filed in . . . but the solemnity of the robed priest, who had already started intoning the Latin chant; the fully dressed officers and EM, who sat quietly, respectfully listening; and the manger scene in the corner of the room . . . hit us like a cold bucket of water.

Suddenly we were as quiet as we were loud before . . . and we looked at ourselves . . . and we felt the degradation we had brought in this house of worship. Under the scornful eyes of the seated occupants, we were trying to back out of the building as quietly as possible when the priest stopped his litany and said 'Wait boys . . . don't go . . . this is where you belong tonight . . . stay and share our celebration of the Christchild.'

[205] While Bob Hope and his USO (United Service Organizations) troupe gave Christmas shows in Vietnam every year from 1964 to 1972, Dau Tieng was too remote to enjoy such a visit and the troops had to make their own entertainment.

We all sat on the back rows of the chapel and, ashamed in our drunkenness, wept like babies . . . because of the season . . . because of our loneliness . . . but most of all because of the kindness of that priest, who did not turn us away.

1967

At Fulton, Missouri on 5 March 1946 Winston Churchill said: 'From Stettin in the Baltic to Trieste in the Adriatic an iron curtain has descended across the Continent.' One of the longest and, in financial terms, most expensive wars in history, the 'Cold War' was fought with great intensity until the Berlin Wall came down in November 1989. Although there were few casualties, both sides took enormous risks in trying to find out what the other was doing. The so-called 'Portland Spy Ring' investigated British submarine technology. Living in suburban Ruislip and posing as an antiquarian book dealer and his wife, Peter and Helen Kroger passed sensitive information to Russia, using microdot technology, radios and sophisticated codes. The group was arrested in January 1961 and, following a high-profile trial, the Krogers received 20-year prison sentences. On 3 January 1968 Prisoner Number 2341 Peter Kroger wrote to their friend, Winnie Myers, from Parkhurst Prison on the Isle of Wight:[206]

Your letter of Dec. 19th, accompanied by my telegram to you, arrived on New Year's Day, which is a very ordinary day in monastic life. Some proposed dates during December had been included in the original draft of the telegram. Having to pass through the hands of several sub-abbots before reaching the Post Office, the dates got lost along the way. A day or two later I sent you a letter (with some comments on Swift) that suggested some dates for visiting. I gathered that business and holiday obligations prevented you from coming over. The dates available throughout January are the 6th — 13th — 20th and 27th on <u>Saturdays</u> and the 7th and 21st on Sundays.[207]

[206] The papers of P. Kroger in the Imperial War Museum Documents Collection: every effort has been made to trace copyright holders and the Imperial War Museum would be grateful for any information which might help to trace those whose identities or addresses are not currently known.

[207] Visitors were expressly forbidden on Good Friday and Christmas Day. The Krogers, both born on the west coast of the United States to parents of Russian or Eastern European extraction, were really Morris Cohen and his wife Lona (nee Petka).

I am delighted to know that Nora, escorted by Sheila and Mary, visited Helen. The last letter from Helen informed me that she was recovering from a virus in the kidneys that had laid her prone for three weeks. We are due for a visit in mid-January which for us will mark the condensation of Christmas, New Year and her 55th birthday into a super-charged couple hours [sic].[208]

Our Christmas in the abbey was remarkably subdued, the quietest I have experienced in my life whether inside or out. We watched 'Scrooge' (starring Alistair Sim) on T.V. over our Xmas pudding. In the evening the Top of the Stars appeared but found it most difficult to draw any resounding laughter. The shroud of melancholy which hung in our common room was too formidable for the artists to break through.

New Year's Day saw us at our ascetic best. It seemed like a touch of life's irony for us to view the film 'The Apartment' in the evening. One of the centrepieces in this film is an eve-of-holiday party in a large office building in which the female employees far exceed the males. Of course the executives, sub-executives and sub-sub-executives all contain 25 genes — and their supreme goal seemed to be for each to possess his own key to the sacrosanct executive toilet.

In October 1969, after serving less than nine years in prison, the Krogers were exchanged with British so-called 'agitator', Gerald Brooke. Helen Kroger died on 23 December 1992 and Peter Kroger died on 23 January 1995.

[208] Prisoner Number 13489 Helen Kroger was held in HM Prison, Parkhurst Road, Holloway, London N7.

1990

At very short notice, Richard Kay, a senior writer with the *Daily Mail*, then serving as the newspaper's Royal Correspondent, flew to Saudi Arabia on 20 December 1990 as an accredited war reporter. He later wrapped a narrative round his despatches from the Gulf:[209]

The following day, Christmas Eve, our numbers by now even more depleted, Ramsay and the Press Association having flown out on the heels of Prince Charles, Chris Buckland and I drove to Jubail to watch the 67th Ordnance Company unload presents and greetings cards for the troops. Back in November commanders complained that the British public were not behind 'our boys'. The response was extraordinary. Tens of thousands of parcels and letters arrived using the BFPO 3000 post code and addressed to simply 'A Soldier', 'A Sailor' or 'An Airman'. There was crate upon crate of what the Army called 'Welfare Goods', perhaps 100 tons in all. They came from cigarette companies, board game manufacturers, toiletry firms and magazine publishers. There were mince pies and Christmas puddings, Mr. Kipling has been exceedingly generous. In addition, for every single soldier, a gift pack from the British Legion. They weren't in truth terribly exciting. Inside each white box was a greeting card, pocket torch, tooth-paste, talcum powder, a frisby and a beer token valid until 1992. But mostly the gifts were from private citizens. The fact that good-natured, generous and kind people took the time and trouble to sit down and write words of friendship to men and women quite unknown to them, struck the troops as evidence of an essential goodness in British life. One soldier alone proudly showed us 90 letters from complete strangers, schoolchildren, housewives and pensioners.

With Christmas Day a traditionally slow news day — normally I would expect my report of the Royal Family's church service and the Queen's Speech to be the main event — turkey and plum pudding with the troops in the front line looked like very good copy indeed. I had hired a four-wheeled drive truck and Chris and I set off for the desert at 5 a.m. At Fadhly we joined up with

[209] *Desert Warrior – Reporting from the Gulf,* published by Penumbra Books in 1992: reprinted by kind permission of the author.

the TV crews, headed by Martin Bell of the BBC and Paul Davis of ITN. A military escort was on hand to rendezvous us with Brigadier Patrick Cordingley, the urbane commander of 7th Brigade. A friendly outgoing man who had won immense respect from his men, his charm belied an inner steeliness. Despite two torpid months in the desert his enthusiasm for his task remained undimmed. The paradox of the occasion, men of war singing carols about peace, was not lost on either of us.

1996

Captain Peter Caddick-Adams, a Territorial Army officer working at the Headquarters of the international Stabilisation Force (SFOR) in Sarajevo, wrote on 27 December to Nigel Steel, Keeper of Documents at the Imperial War Museum:[210]

Christmas morning dawned with not a flake of snow in sight. We'd had some earlier in December, & plenty of the white stuff was forecast, but so far, our gathering of the world's most qualified military meteorological experts had failed to come up with the goods. I had reasoned that if there was one place on earth that one could guarantee a white Christmas, it would be Sarajevo. First call of the day was to our headquarters on the far side of the city for a Festival of Nine Lessons and Carols. Organised by our transatlantic cousins, the service was in fact a competition to cram in as many carols as possible — the final tally was fourteen, at which point my voice gave out. The cousins changed the tunes of several favourites, & introduced a new carol to me, to the tune of Greensleeves *(thumbs down). The congregation were the English speakers of SFOR, & included a few brave Germans & Dutch. Americans have a thing about singing holding lighted candles, so we provided a fair rendering of* Silent Night *to the accompaniment of burning hymn-sheets, treading the hot wax into the carpet. Events like this have to be recorded by US television, & I must admit I got rather irritated by the pop of flash bulbs in my face as I tried to put meaning into* See Amidst the Winter's Snow*, but a glance outside confirmed that there was still none of the white stuff.*

Christmas Eve's service was memorable by some excellent Handel & Mozart on the Cathedral organ, & singing Stille Nacht, Heilige Nacht, *in candlelight. It's one carol that sounds so much better in its original German, and has echoes of communal singing in the trenches, during the 1914 Christmas Truce. German camera crews recorded the service & I gather I made*

---

[210] The papers of Captain P. Caddick-Adams TD in the Imperial War Museum Documents Collection: every effort has been made to trace copyright holders and the author and the Imperial War Museum would be grateful for any information which might help to trace those whose identities or addresses are not currently known.

an appearance on Christmas Day television in the Fatherland, alongside the singing Oberfeldwebels . . .

    Time for Christmas lunch. First, in time honoured tradition, serve the chaps — not many of them as this HQ is all chiefs and no Indians. Then the generals (no shortage of them) served us. Catering for so many nationalities, the menus were rather mixed up, and I ended up with a plate of roast beef, turkey, ham, mint sauce, and chips . . . On to pudding, and the (Bosnian) chefs had made an outstanding effort with the British Christmas pud — done to a crisp . . . A pneumatic drill was required to tackle the outer case, and a drinking straw the interior, which was as molten lava. A glance outside, and yes, the white stuff was tumbling down, and by evening a very respectable four inches had accumulated. Her Majesty's annual broadcast being sadly unavailable, I made do with a showing of Independence Day, *& a bucket of popcorn, courtesy of the cousins, in the office next to mine — yes, we carried on working, and in uniform. Being predominantly Muslim, the city carried on too. I spotted just one Christmas tree, and two festively-dressed shop windows in a walk around town on Christmas Eve; rather a refreshing change from an English high street at this time of year. No invitations to challenge the national debt, or over-consume. Unfortunately, the Christmas spirit did not dissuade some fundamentalist Muslims in Sarajevo from deciding that Santa Claus threatened Islam, and that the solution was to mug any Croat Father Christmases they encountered.*

2006

On 24 December 2006 Raymond Whitaker wrote in *The Independent*:[211]

Today, somewhere in Iraq or Afghanistan, at least one Christmas dinner is likely to be held. It will be a curious mixture of khaki camouflage and silly hats, bits of tinsel and no-nonsense weaponry. British forces on operational duties have to celebrate Christmas when they can, and for some, that will not be on Christmas Day. Even for those who do not have to go on patrol or guard duty, or form part of the rapid-reaction force, which is on standby to deal with emergencies, tomorrow will not be a day of leisure.

This morning, troops will be able to hear a special Christmas message from the Queen, in which she tells them: 'Your courage and loyalty are not lightly taken . . . and I know that yours is a job which often calls for great personal risk. This year men and women from across the armed forces have lost their lives in action in both Iraq and Afghanistan.'

Troops in both theatres will be hoping to hear from their families, who get an extra 30 free minutes in phone calls at Christmas, courtesy of what is called the 'operations welfare package'. Their loved ones in uniform will probably have a parcel from home to open — for six weeks before Christmas, families can send packages weighing up to 2.2kg without charge. At this time of year, the Postal Courier Squadron in southern Iraq deals with 1,000 bags of parcels a night.

All of Britain's 25,000 troops abroad, wherever they are, will also benefit from a tradition which has its origins in 1914. Two years ago the tradition was revived, and tomorrow each soldier, sailor, airman or woman overseas will receive a red decorated box with £35-worth of goodies inside. The contents are secret, but last year the box had some novelties, snacks and toiletries, and this year, according to Captain Gary Hedges, a military spokesman in Basra, it is 'bigger and better'.

Also aiming to achieve a surprise will be the cooks in places like Helmand's Camp Bastion and Basra province's Shaibah logistics base. They will be up as early as 3am tomorrow to prepare something special for the day, the nature of which is always a closely guarded secret. At one base

[211] © *The Independent*: reproduced with permission.

in Helmand this Christmas, they received a surprise of their own: celebrity chef Gordon Ramsay flew in to join them in cooking a turkey dinner with all the trimmings for 800 troops. In some of the more out-of-the-way dangerous bases, the catering staff will have to improvise with whatever they get their hands on locally. But they will all endeavour to produce something as close as possible to a traditional Christmas feast.

'Every cookhouse has a Christmas tree,' said Capt Hedges. This is something of a surprise to anyone who has been to Helmand or Basra province, since there is scarcely a stick of vegetation in either region. 'Oh no, they're not real,' he continued. 'They are made of wire and plastic. They come as part of the welfare package.'

2006

Graham Hesketh was born in Liverpool on 1 December 1971 and grew up at Runcorn in Cheshire. He was educated at Our Lady's Junior School, where he was an altar boy in the local Catholic Church, and later at St. Chad's School. After leaving school he joined the Royal Tank Regiment, serving for three years in Germany, Northern Ireland and Cyprus. Having left the Army in 1992, he found that he couldn't settle down in civilian life and re-enlisted in 1995, this time joining his local regiment, The King's (Liverpool) Regiment. During the next decade Graham Hesketh saw service in former Yugoslavia, Canada, Jordan, Northern Ireland, Kenya and Germany.

On 11 November 2006 Sergeant Hesketh deployed to Iraq as a highly-experienced Platoon Sergeant with the 2nd Battalion, The Duke of Lancaster's Regiment, with which his former regiment had merged four months earlier. He saw his fiancée, Rebecca Barnes, a technician serving with the same battalion, on Boxing Day, after which he wrote her a short note:[212]

Hi babes,

I'm just sat in the back of a Warrior *waiting to come back to see you. I really love you and am missing you like mad and it's you babe, I never want to be away from you again. I want to spend the rest of my life with you. I so want us to be together till the day I die. You are my world and I am so glad I met you. I want us to have family of our own. You do me proud. I know I have met the soulmate to my life and I never want to lose you ever. I will sign off now babe and hopefully I will see you when I get back.*

All my love,

Graham

[212] Published by kind permission of Corporal Rebecca Barnes.

Two days later Sergeant Graham Hesketh's *Warrior* tracked armoured vehicle was destroyed by an improvised explosive device as the patrol returned to its base, the Old State Building, in the centre of Basra. Sergeant Hesketh died from his injuries while being evacuated to the Military Field Hospital at Shaibah Logistics Base. He was the 127th British soldier to lose his life in Iraq since the invasion in 2003. By a previous relationship Graham Hesketh left Georgia, aged seven, and Ben, aged three.